LEADERSHIP EXCELLENCE IN ORGANIZATIONAL ESSENTIALS

DR GAJANAN SHIRKE

Made with ❤ on the Notion Press Platform
www.notionpress.com

I would like to express a special debt of gratitude to my wife Rajeshree and my two daughters Rupeshi & Kavya, my teammates and superior leaders who encourages me to write.

Contents

About Book

This book makes a much needed contribution to what young leaders know about the Essential role and work. Organizational behavior refers to the research and study of behavior of human beings in a structured setting of an organization. It also includes the study of the behavior of the organization and how it functions. This field has three main sub branches of research namely macro-level organizational behavior, micro-level organizational behavior and meso level work group behavior. This book unfolds the innovative aspects of organizational behavior, which will be crucial for the holistic understanding of the subject matter. The topics covered in this extensive text deal with the core aspects of this field. The textbook is appropriate for those seeking detailed information in this area.

About The Author

Dr Gajanan Shirke, a hotel consultant, has years of extensive experience in the hospitality industry. His thirst for learning and aspiration to become a multi-faceted expert in the hotel industry helped him rise from employment to becoming an independent professional in the hospitality sector. Since his last assignment as General Manager at Kamat Hotels, he has become a renowned hotel consultant with a proven track record of developing, training and growing some of the best-known hotels, restaurants and fast-food joints in the Indian market. He was appointed as an expert consultant for The Eighth meeting of the Board of Studies for Hotel Management & Catering Technology. He is a visiting faculty at various Hotel Management Colleges and has trained over a thousand hospitality professionals. He has completed numerous pre and post opening hotel consultancies in India and overseas.

In order to spread his extensive knowledge to aspiring hotel professionals, Gajanan has penned a large number of books spanning different segments of the hospitality industry. Starting from his first book 'Bar Management and Operations' published in 2010, he has written 47 books including Hospitality Management, Food and Beverage Management, Hotel Engineering Management, Front Office Management, Hotel Housekeeping Management, The Cookery Trilogy: Advance Cookery Theory, The Cookery Trilogy: Foundation of Cookery, The Cookery Trilogy: The Basic Cookery Book, Hotel Sales and Marketing, Hospitality Industry Accounting & Fundamentals, Customer Interaction Excellence in Hospitality, History of Indian Cuisine – Volume 1, History of Indian Cuisine – Volume 2, Hotel Owner's Manual, Hotel Security & Prevention, Training Manager's Manual, Exceptional Service In Hospitality Six Sigma Way, etc.

Index

CHAPTER ONE

Appreciate Inquiry

Appreciative inquiry (AI) is a positive approach to leadership development and organizational change. The method is used to boost innovation among organizations. A company might apply appreciative inquiry to best practices, strategic planning, organizational culture, and to increase the momentum of initiatives. This approach has also been applied at the societal level for discussion on topics of global importance. For example, non-profit and non-governmental organizations (NGOs) might design initiatives across global regions and industry sectors after analysis using appreciative inquiry.

The fundamental idea behind AI is that over time, it has become increasingly common for organizations to approach change and growth from a problem-solving perspective. As firms aim to improve efficiency, survive, perform better, and boost competitiveness, AI proponents argue that there has come to be an unhealthy over-emphasis on fixing what's wrong a deficit-based approach. AI arose as a challenge to these ingrained assumptions and proposed that organizations can benefit instead from what is called a strengths-based or affirmative approach. This affirmative approach, in turn, assumes that each human system has a positive core of strengths. This positive core is not vastly different from the way we view organizational strengths in conventional management literature. In essence (and loosely paraphrased from the authors), they can be seen to encompass:

- The values, beliefs, and capabilities of our organization when it's 'at its best'; and
- Collective understandings around what makes up the best of us.

As a concept in positive organizational psychology, AI is probably best understood by looking at its evolution over time.

The 5D Cycle of Appreciative Inquiry:

Definition (Clarifying): The first step in an Appreciative Inquiry process is defining the central question or topic of the inquiry, dialogue, or engagement process. The definition phase establishes the scope and goals of the inquiry. Importantly, AI emphasizes a positive, solutions-oriented approach to defining the process. While a more traditional "problem-solving" process might begin with collecting data and diagnosing weaknesses, AI begins with positive, asset-based framing questions to determine what's already working in a community, organization, or team.

Discovery (Appreciating): In the second step of an Appreciative Inquiry process, participants engage in a dialogue designed to surface the most positive features of a community, organization, or team. By beginning with positively framed questions, participants discuss and come to appreciate what's already working. This task is accomplished by focusing on peak times of organizational excellence, when people have experienced the organization as most alive and effective. Seeking to understand the unique factors (e.g., leadership, relationships, technologies, core processes, structures, values, learning processes, external relationships, planning methods, and so on) that made the high points possible, people deliberately 'let go' of analyses of deficits and systematically seek to isolate and learn from even the smallest wins. In some presentations of the model, the Discovery step is divided into two phases: the first phase is to identify and discuss positive, effective, or exceptional moments, events, or periods of success, and the second phase is to look for themes or common elements among those positive moments, events, and successes.

Life Giving Forces: In the parlance of the AI community, these moments and themes are sometimes called "Life Giving Forces" (or LGFs), which the Center for Appreciative Inquiry defines as "elements or experiences within the organization's past and/or present that represent the organization's strengths when it is operating at its very best."

Positive Core: Another common term in the AI community, the "Positive Core" refers to the central assets of community, organization, or team. AI has demonstrated that human systems grow in the direction of their persistent inquiries, and this propensity is strongest and most sustainable when the means and ends of inquiry are positively correlated. In the AI process, the future is consciously constructed upon the positive core strengths of the organization."

Dream (Envisioning): In the third step of an Appreciative Inquiry process, participants collaboratively envision a desired future for their community, organization, or team. One aspect that differentiates AI from other visioning or planning methodologies is that images of the future emerge out of grounded examples from its positive past. Rather than imagining hypothetical strategies to address past problems, AI asks participants to consciously envision a preferred future that is grounded in past successes but imaginatively and creatively unrestrained.

Provocative Proposition: In the AI community, a "Provocative Proposition" refers to a collectively produced statement or, in some cases, a graphic or illustration that captures the outcome of the dreaming/envisioning process. According to the Center for Appreciative Inquiry, "The provocative proposition bridges the best of 'what is' with your/their own speculation or intuition of 'what might be.' It is provocative to the extent that it stretches the realm of the status quo, challenges common assumptions or routines, and helps suggest real possibilities that represent desired possibilities for the individual, group, or organization." In some AI processes, Provocative Propositions are used (or also used) in the Design phase and are sometimes called *Possibility Propositions* They bridge 'the best of what is' (identified in *Discovery*) with 'what might be' (imagined in *Dream*).

Design (Co-Constructing): In the fourth step of an Appreciative Inquiry process, participants begin to co-constructively design a new or refashioned community, organization, or team. While participants imagined possibilities in the Dream stage, they start to assemble the practical elements of a plan in the Design stage.

Deliver/Destiny (Innovating): The final step in an Appreciative Inquiry process is the implementation of the collective design. In his original formulations of the model, Delivery evoked images of traditional change-management implementation. Importantly, the Center for Appreciative Inquiry notes that during this phase communities, organizations, or teams innovate and improvise ways to create the preferred future by continuously improvising and building AI competencies into the culture, which includes noticing and celebrating successes that are moving the system toward the preferred future the organization or group co-created.

Principles of Appreciative Inquiry:

1. **Constructionist Principle (Words Create Worlds):** Reality, as we know it, is a subjective vs. objective state and is socially created through language and conversations.
2. **Simultaneity Principle(Inquiry Creates Change):** The moment we ask a question, we begin to create a change. The questions we ask are fateful.
3. **PoeticPrinciple(We Can Choose What We Study):** Teams and organizations, like open books, are endless sources of study and learning. What we choose to study makes a difference. It describes—even creates—the world as we know it.
4. **AnticipatoryPrinciple(Images Inspire Action):** Human systems move in the direction of their images of the future. The more positive and hopeful the image of the future, the more positive the present-day action.
5. **Positive Principle(Positive Questions Lead to Positive Change):** Momentum for small- or large-scale change requires large amounts of positive affect and social bonding. This momentum is best generated through positive questions that amplify the positive core.

Criticisms of Appreciative Inquiry: Several criticisms of the Appreciative Inquiry model have emerged over the years, but the most salient and widely discussed tend to focus on (1) the lack of strong evidence supporting the model's efficacy and (2) the model's emphasis on positivity. In addition, the evangelical manner and idolatry of some practitioners in the AI community, as well as the community's sometimes quasi-mystical language, have made some observers skeptical of both the AI process and the objectivity of the AI community. When theoretical, conceptual, or procedural models are applied in community, organization, or team processes, the efficacy of a given model will depend on the quality of implementation, which can encompass a wide range of complex factors that can positively or negatively impact outcomes (e.g.: Was the facilitation strong or weak? Did the facilitators understand the model and did they maintain fidelity to the model? Was a sufficient amount of time allocated for the process? Or was the process rushed? Etc.). Consequently, it is often difficult to determine what may have gone right or wrong with the application of a given model or process.

In some cases, critics of AI claim that positive transformational change is unlikely to take hold in a community, organization, or team if problems are ignored, overlooked, and left unaddressed, though proponents of AI would argue that "deficit-based" processes also have their own problems and downsides, including ample evidence that more traditional problem-oriented approaches also routinely fail to result in positive transformational change. One compelling argument against AI's emphasis on positivity, however, is that community, organization, or team leaders may use AI's positive framing to shutting down discussion of problems. In this case, for example, an organization's directors may have a vested interest in avoiding discussions of problems in the organization because leadership quality may be cited as one of the organization's biggest problems. AI does not necessarily exclude all forms of negativity, and AI processes can be designed to frame discussions of problems in ways that are "generative" and productive. Perhaps the most potentially problematic dimension of Appreciative Inquiry's positive framing is that an AI process may be used in ways that reinforce and perpetuate racial or cultural bias, prejudice, and discrimination. By insisting that an inquiry, dialogue, or engagement process focus exclusively on positive questions, comments, and ideas, for example, the AI process can potentially be used—intentionally or unintentionally—in ways that silence legitimate concerns and criticisms raised by the victims of bias, prejudice, and discrimination. When applied to equity-based dialogues or engagement processes, AI's perceived prohibition on negativity raises both serious and well-founded concerns, given that silencing legitimate anger, frustration, and complaints is a ubiquitous feature of inequitable, discriminatory, and oppressive systems. Consequently, engagement professionals and practitioners should be mindful of their cultural biases and motivations when facilitating AI-based processes, especially in diverse communities and workplaces, and they should consider adaptations that do not stifle necessary discussions about uncomfortable or troubling issues such as racial prejudice, gender discrimination, or workplace abuse.

Determining What Could and Should Be: The Navy introduced Appreciative Inquiry through a series of interviews from the bottom-up within its hierarchal structure. The goal of the interview process wasn't merely to ask about the Navy's problems and how to solve them but to inquire as to what represented the best of the Navy from each interviewee. The Navy's approach was to combine the best values of the organization with asking *what should be* and envision *what could be*. Instead of viewing the Navy as a problem that needed to be solved, the goal shifted to a "what can be" strategy.

360-Degree Feedback: The Navy used a 360-degree feedback method to draw on each person's knowledge that included multi-dimensional leadership. It's focused on each person's circle of influence, such as the direct reports, peers, and supervisors, to help create a shared vision of the Navy's leadership needed in the future. After identifying the vision, they generated ideas and the needed changes to create and implement that vision. Creating an alignment between everyone involved empowered the participants by bringing forward ideas and change initiatives, which altered the discussion from negative to positive feedback. Leadership stories were gathered and allowed people to relate to each other and embrace different kinds of leadership that all participants desired within the Navy. Through an analysis of all of the feedback, the change initiatives centered around several concepts, including the autonomy to act for those serving in the Navy, attention to personal needs, the types of risks leaders take, and teamwork.

Co-creating With Stakeholders Including Customers: If modern leadership is all about asking questions, those questions need to be asked with, and answered by, all the stakeholders in a system. By engaging the diverse voices in an organization, leaders can lift up the wisdom that is distributed across their system. Doing so not only leads to more robust solutions; it also helps build commitment for those solutions, because people commit to what they help co-create. Organizations that are successfully pivoting amid the pandemic realize that this engagement extends to employees and customers. Bringing the customer voice into processes helps inform the customer while keeping the organization close to what customers want and need as the world changes. The principle of wholeness from AI reminds leaders that change is always more effective when the whole system is engaged.

Prototyping and Pivoting: It is also important to begin turning the ideas generated through inquiry and stakeholder engagement into action. One way to do so is by prototyping and pivoting. Rather than waiting for the perfect new product or process, leaders can roll out beta tests and experiment with pilot projects. Getting concepts "out there" for people to see and interact with helps leaders move away from the old mindset that a change initiative is neat and tidy. Instead, they can lean into a continual reinvention mindset where they take action, learn from it and pivot to the next iteration.

CHAPTER TWO

Business Acumen

Business Acumen is a combination of knowledge and skill informed by experience: knowledge about key business issues, the skill to apply that knowledge, and the confidence to take action informed by past experiences. The ability to take a 'big picture' view of a situation, to weigh it up quickly, make a logical, sound decision confidently, and influence others to agree with you in order to have a positive impact towards achieving the objectives of the organisation. This definition was created as a starting point for debate with our clients, because everyone will have a slightly different view depending on their own experience and the market context they manage. But overall, most definitions express the capabilities of people with a certain mix of skills including

Financial literacy – The ability to understand how an organisation uses its resources to achieve its desired outcome. In a commercial context, this is often measured in terms of profit or revenue, in other organisations the key measure of success might be improved capacity or measurable social benefits.

Organisational knowledge – Knowledge about the organisation in which the individual works. What are the relevant procedures and processes? How can they get things done?

Ability to deal with ambiguity – In many cases, it is impossible to know everything relevant to a situation. Each individual must decide when the information available is sufficient to move forward.

Ability to link cause and effect – Both in a financial sense e.g. 10% discount means we will not make a profit, and in a personal sense e.g. if we don't complete this forecast accurately, our boss will not secure the resources we need next year.

Self-Awareness – How will an individual's actions and decisions impact on the organisation and the other people in it?

Stakeholder Awareness – What are the stakeholder's interests and needs, and how do decisions made within the organisation impact upon them?

Contextual Knowledge – The ability to relate what happens outside an individual's immediate environment to situations in the workplace. For senior managers, this will involve looking at the wider external landscape. For supervisors, it means knowing about the changes happening within their own organisation.

Some people believe business acumen is a skill reserved for senior leaders. However, in order to become a senior leader you need to have developed acumen. What's more today's challenges require agility at all levels of the organisation and so having skill lower down the organisation is advantageous. Why is this? Organisations in all sectors, public, private and the third are under increasing pressure and need to be more agile. We see recurring factors such as:

- The increasingly extreme and unpredictable nature of changes in the external and internal environment.
- The necessity to react and make decisions quickly often with limited and incomplete information and at lower levels in the organisation.
- Organisational structures becoming increasingly complex, with outsourcing models and elongated supply chains becoming more complex too.
- And finally, we hear more and more companies say that success is more directly linked to an individual relying not just on technical skills, but on the ability to understand the wider organisational context.

Business acumen skills

What skills can help leaders build business acumen? It's more than just business knowledge. Here are eight skills that contribute to someone's business acumen.

Strategic thinking and problem-solving: Coming up with effective plans designed to reach company goals is a key component of business acumen. Strategic planning and problem-solving contribute to this ability. You also need to know how to prioritize according to a variety of situations. Not all priorities will be the same at all times. Leaders need to use their strategic thinking to figure it out on the go. They must also be able to adapt and solve problems creatively. Adapting to change is necessary for an organization to thrive in any market. Previous solutions may not always get a team the same results. But someone with business acumen can think on their feet.

Leadership: Someone with business acumen should also possess strong leadership skills and characteristics. They can inspire others to meet the needs of the organization. A capable leader can prioritize and adapt those priorities to keep the focus on what matters most, even amid change.

Comfort with the numbers: It's important to understand processes and financial metrics like budgeting, forecasting, profit and loss, and reporting, just to name a few. Being comfortable with these numbers helps someone take the pulse of an organization. It's also important to know the basics of reading a P&L, balance sheet, and cash flow statement.

Other important number factors to know about include:

How a company drives its cash flow

The basics of operations in your company and which parts are the biggest levers of performance and growth

What is unique about your operations?

What affects the bottom line?

Communication and influence: Communication is a crucial skill that makes up business acumen. It's important to know how to communicate effectively with others to help everyone function more effectively. Someone with business acumen also understands what matters to different audiences and stakeholders. They know how to communicate a compelling vision and explain the why behind it.

These communication skills can be used to develop relationships in your project or team to create better outcomes.

Marketing: Someone with business savvy knows their target audience. But they should also understand how to discover who that target audience is. They also know how to come up with key marketing angles to attract that audience. In addition, they need to know KPIs to track and measure growth. This doesn't mean you need to be a marketing expert to have business acumen. But having a grasp on the basics is part of building acumen skills.

Analytical capabilities: Analytical capabilities are key to business acumen. These can include:

Collecting and analyzing information

Connecting the dots between data points

Understand a problem from different angles

Understanding what information is rare and valuable and the limitations of what is available

Understanding the market: Understanding your market is not the same as having marketing skills. It involves understanding the industry you work in and what the marketplace looks like. For instance, someone who understands the market knows how to do a competitive analysis, how to track and follow industry trends, and ultimately how to pivot when the market demands.

Context and situational awareness: Someone with business acumen knows how their actions affect the organization they work for in a variety of situations. They have the emotional intelligence to understand how team members feel about a given situation and are equipped to handle it accordingly.

Developing business acumen

Because business acumen is in high demand in the workforce, people who have it can make a big difference for their organization. Here is how someone in your organization can develop business acumen and become an asset for their team and the company at large.

Dig into the financial side of the business: It's important to become financially literate in the business sense. But this doesn't happen on its own. Even someone who is naturally good with numbers won't automatically understand a company's financial side without digging into it.

Some examples of how someone can improve their financial literacy in an organization include:

Tracking important metrics over time

Getting insight from business intelligence data

Looking at financial statements

Asking for help if there are metrics you don't understand

Get a mentor: Anyone who wants to grow their skills in a given industry should find someone willing to mentor them. This person should have the strong business acumen skills you want to develop. Mentors can provide a much-needed perspective that someone on their own cannot access. Their deeper knowledge and experience in the organization give them an advantage that they can pass on to their mentee. However, with reverse mentoring, the mentor is not always the senior member in this exchange. Young employees have a valuable perspective and set of experiences they can convey to their older peers.

Study the business model: Studying the company's business model can help an employee learn about areas of business they don't know much about yet. It can also help them understand growth strategies used by the business. For instance, how does the supply chain work? How does the company handle its human resource management? Understanding the business model can help someone see the big picture.

Stay up to date with industry trends: Business acumen isn't an evergreen skill. Anyone who wants to develop and upkeep business acumen should stay up to date with industry trends.

Some ways to do this include:

Following business leaders on social media

Subscribing to newsletters in your industry

Keeping up with business news

If you want to build more business acumen, start doing your research and make a habit of it. Those who want to encourage others in their organization to develop business acumen can encourage them to develop this habit, as well.

Understand the customers: Anyone who wants to know more about a business should talk to customers when they can. Talking directly to customers is the best way to get their perspective on the organization you work for. It's also a great way to collect their feedback and improve business performance. Study customer satisfaction with your organization's Net Promoter Score (NPS) and Customer Satisfaction Score (CSAT). Customer data doesn't give you the customer's unique perspective, but it does provide the big picture of who the customers are.

Sign up for a business class: Taking a business class can be a more structured way to develop competencies that help improve business acumen. Reading a quick overview book can also help people jumpstart the process of building business acumen. Do you want to support business acumen development in your organization? Make sure to invest in professional development courses for your employees. When building business acumen, self-driven learning is key.

Become more comfortable taking calculated risks: Practicing business acumen requires taking risks. No risk means no reward. It can feel uncomfortable at first to take risks. Encourage people in your organization to take smaller risks first if this scares them.

Learn how to fail: If you want to achieve success, you'll have to encounter failure along the way. Learn how to make "good failures." Good failures aren't based on sloppiness or failing to ask for help. Instead, they're designed to help you and others learn as much as possible. Learn how to pick yourself up after your failures. If you can learn from them and move on, you're already steps ahead.

Invest in coaching: A coach can help people speed up the process of developing their business acumen. Should someone get a coach if they already have a mentor? You can benefit from getting both. Consider bringing in skilled coaches to help people in your organization build their business acumen, even if there's already a healthy culture of mentorship.

Showcasing your business acumen skills: If you're someone who's developed business acumen skills over the years, how you showcase them matters almost just as much as how you use them. Showcasing your business acumen can help organizations understand your worth. This is true whether you're planning your career in the same organization or if you're looking for opportunities elsewhere. Include specific skills in your resume. For example, add analytical skills if you have them. Give examples of how you've used those skills in the past to succeed in a previous position. You should also be prepared to talk about business considerations (of your former employer and your prospective one) relative to the role you want.

Develop business acumen and become an asset to your organization: If you see yourself evolving as a leader in an organization, it's crucial that you develop business acumen sooner rather than later. But you don't have to figure it out alone. Coaches at BetterUp can help you awaken your potential and become the leader with the necessary business acumen to make transformational decisions. Try out a custom demo to get started.

BUSINESS ACUMEN IMPACT

Everywhere! The core tenets of business acumen emphasize a need to think outside the confines of individual actions, siloed departmental decisions, and short-term gains. Seeing the big picture at all times changes how people think and behave - in turn, changing how the organization operates.

Day-to-day Operations: Organizations that prioritize business acumen provide a clearer vision and an overall context within which employees can work, while creating an environment that is more likely to break down internal barriers. There is less waste and less ambivalence. There is increased innovation. Employees are more engaged, they understand their role and its impact on business results, and they are more likely to believe that their efforts really matter. They are more likely to think like a business owner.

Budgeting and Forecasting: When an individual has a keen understanding of their organization's goals, metrics like Return on Sales (ROS) and how to budget and forecast within those parameters, they will make well-informed business decisions.

Buying and Selling: Understanding Cost of Goods Sold (COGS) and Gross Profit Margin (GPM) will have a large impact on how organizations negotiate with vendors and how their sales professionals work with clients. A sales professional's understanding of targeted GPM will allow them to leverage their price setting latitude and mold their client dialog. Being able to position their product or service as having the potential to improve their client's GPM changes the dynamic from simply buying and selling. They're empowering their clients to make informed, business-savvy decisions.

EMPOWER YOUR ORGANIZATION WITH BUSINESS ACUMEN

You train. And one method of training stands head and shoulders above the rest - learning by doing, whether in-person, live in a virtual classroom, or in an asynchronous simulation. Confucius said it best I hear and I forget. I see and I remember. I do and I understand. First, business acumen training has to be engaging and energizing enough to overcome the "oh no" factor typically associated with any training that is "financial." Making it palatable to possibly reluctant learners and maximizing participant engagement is key. You can achieve this in-person, virtually and through gamified simulations.

Second, it can't overwhelm and frustrate learners by going beyond the needs of the audience. Three days of training around financial terms and statements, for example, is generally not necessary for those who aren't in finance jobs. Having flexible offerings is key depending on the audience. Some audiences may prefer a full day, while others may do better with half. Others may want a self-paced environment. Flexibility is key. Since the focus of business acumen training for managers is, of necessity, at a higher level than most skill-based development, relevance also is essential. It's not just about learning specific skills, but about driving insights about the enterprise as a whole. Can the learners take the experience and apply it directly and immediately to their role in strengthening the financial performance of the company?

Finally, it needs to be memorable. The knowledge gained from more interactive learning experiences far surpasses that of traditional, lecture-based training because it's sticky. According to some estimates, employees retain 75% of what they learn when they practice while learning. Creating a gamified, built-in practice environment is key to walking away feeling confident to apply your learnings to your job.

CHAPTER THREE

Business Ethics

Ethics refer to the desirable and appropriate values and morals according to an individual or the society at large. Ethics deal with the purity of individuals and their intentions. Ethics serve as guidelines for analyzing what is good or bad in a specific scenario. Correlating ethics with leadership, we find that ethics is all about the leader's identity and the leader's role.

Ethical theories on leadership talk about two main things: (a) The actions and behaviour of leaders; and (b) the personality and character of leaders. It is essential to note that "Ethics are an essential to leadership". A leader drives and influences the subordinates / followers to achieve a common goal, be it in case of team work, organizational quest, or any project. It is an ethical job of the leader to treat his subordinates with respect as each of them has unique personality. The ethical environment in an organization is built and developed by a leader as they have an influential role in the organization and due to the fact that leaders have an influence in developing the organizational values.

An effective and ethical leader has the following traits / characteristics:

Dignity and respectfulness: He respects others. An ethical leader should not use his followers as a medium to achieve his personal goals. He should respect their feelings, decision and values. Respecting the followers implies listening effectively to them, being compassionate to them, as well as being liberal in hearing opposing viewpoints. In short, it implies treating the followers in a manner that authenticate their values and beliefs.

Serving others: He serves others. An ethical leader should place his follower's interests ahead of his interests. He should be humane. He must act in a manner that is always fruitful for his followers.

Justice: He is fair and just. An ethical leader must treat all his followers equally. There should be no personal bias. Wherever some followers are treated differently, the ground for differential treatment should be fair, clear, and built on morality.

Community building: He develops community. An ethical leader considers his own purpose as well as his followers' purpose, while making efforts to achieve the goals suitable to both of them. He is considerate to the community interests. He does not overlook the followers' intentions. He works harder for the community goals.

Honesty: He is loyal and honest. Honesty is essential to be an ethical and effective leader. Honest leaders can be always relied upon and depended upon. They always earn respect of their followers. An honest leader presents the fact and circumstances truly and completely, no matter how critical and harmful the fact may be. He does not misrepresent any fact.

It is essential to note that leadership is all about values, and it is impossible to be a leader if you lack the awareness and concern for your own personal values. Leadership has a moral and ethical aspect. These ethics define leadership. Leaders can use the above mentioned traits as yardsticks for influencing their own behaviour.

Optimizes brand image: The ethical leadership of an organization is quite effective in showing the best that a brand has and hence, it optimizes the brand's reputation.

Enhances emotional well-being: Ethical leadership is quite effective in channelizing a stress-free and constructive work environment that optimizes the emotional well-being of the employees and improves organizational efficiency.

Traits of Leaders who make Ethical Decisions: Ethical leaders will not let wrongful behavior and actions slide. Even if such activities benefit the organization, they ensure never to compromise company morals.

Traits of ethical leaders-

Leads by example

Willing to evolve

Respects everyone equally

Communicates openly

Manages stress effectively

Mediates fairly

Key Elements of Ethical Leadership

Leading by example: In ethical leadership, leaders are supposed to lead their teams by their own ethical activities. Behaving in an honest, ethical, and unselfish manner is pivotal in setting examples for the subordinates.

This way leaders also gain the respect of their team members.

Championing the Importance of Ethics: Ethical leadership also incorporates an absolute focus upon ethics by following ethical standards in all activities. They also pay heed to ethical issues and ensure how their as well as organizational behavior would influence society.

Communicating: Being a good communicator is also integral to ethical leadership culture in an organization. Leaders should not only be able to communicate well, plus others should also not be scared of speaking to them.

The six principles according to the FATHER framework are

Fairness – It suggests treating others fairly and having an organizational culture where everyone treats others with fairness.

Accountability – Ethical leadership suggests that leaders should also take accountability for their bad decisions or mistakes.

Trust – For building great relationships and teams, ethical leadership utilizes mutual trust-building.

Honesty – It is important for leaders who want to follow an ethical style of leadership to understand that honesty is the best policy.

Equality – When it comes to following leadership ethics, following the principle of equality is its backbone which is also integral to global human survival and bliss.

Respect – In ethical leadership, respect is associated with showing regard to other's perceptions, rights, wishes, feelings, orientations, etc.

What Causes Ethical Failures?

According to the author and ethical leadership expert Linda Fisher Thornton, two types of causes behind ethical failures can be-

- **Individual causes-** It revolves around ignoring boundaries such as organizational values or industry codes, lack of self-control, or following the crowd
- **Organizational causes-** It revolves around a lack of positive role models, lack of accountability, or the lack of codified standards of behavior and training

Some of the steps that can help you become a leader who follows ethics

Defined Organisation's Values: An ethical leader sets the vision of the organization. This vision is deeply rooted in the philosophies, morals, ethics, and values of the organization. The idea of a company is the ultimate goal they want to achieve, but what about day-to-day functioning? An ethical leader ensures that people uphold the company's core values even in the daily functioning of the business. After setting the organization's goals, the leader must convey the same to the team members.

Be Aware of your Values: Good leaders are in touch with their values and virtues and understand the organization's values and goals. Ethical leaders never compromise on their morals, and as a result, they ensure to behave in ways that maintain their morals while upholding company values.

Set the Tone: The ethical leader creates an environment that fosters such morals and values. They set the tone of conduct, behavior, and the mindset of the organization. A way to do this is to be a good role model to others in the business. Actions have consequences, which may be the driving force of an ethical leader's behavior. These consequences set the standard of conduct that they will follow—both positive and negative consequences matter. Positive consequences matter as well and act as a reward for good behavior.

Identify Ethical Dilemmas: An ethical leader should be an expert at recognizing ethical dilemmas. These situations may not include an outright lie but may be a misinterpretation of reality. Whatever the case may be, it is not the absolute truth.

Ethical dilemmas may arise due to purchasing, hiring, firing, calculating bonuses, promoting, etc. The best way to recognize an ethical dilemma is to listen to the inner voice that tells you whether you are right or wrong.

Dealing with Ethical Dilemmas:Identifying ethical dilemmas is another key step here. Once an ethical leader recognizes a moral dilemma, it is essential to do damage control. There are various ways of responding to the ethical dilemmas:

Be Prepared: Creating possible scenarios can help one work to react if such a situation arises. This allows the team to prepare for a crisis because it is necessary to be ready to decide in a matter of minutes in such a scenario.

Gather Evidence: Evidence of unethical behavior should be gathered so that it can be verified. This is necessary to determine what action should be taken.

Reevaluate your decision: If you come up with a decision, pause, rethink the same. No ethical leader can afford to make a hasty decision. The wrong decision may have disastrous consequences.

Seek Advice: An ethical leader will gain others' advice and input to understand and evaluate the situation more rationally. This helps them earn multiple points of view on the same matter. As a result, they can recognize and deal with such dilemmas effectively.

Have Courage: An ethical leader must have the courage to take a stand for what's true when maybe lying or manipulating is the simpler choice. Such a decision requires the maker of the decision to be risky and bold. Sometimes the choices made by an ethical leader are the harder alternative, or it is the unpopular choice. Even in such a situation, the ethical leader must persevere and stay on the side of integrity, morality, and honesty.

Ethical Leadership Behaviors to Practice

Set an Example: Ethical leaders, like any other leaders, are the model example of behavior and conduct in any organization. Through their conduct, they set an example for others in the organization. As a result, a leader trying to follow the ethical leadership style must work towards being a worthy example for others in an organization to look up to. Ethical leaders also expect that managers and members alike lead by example.

Be Vocal About the Importance of Ethics: People who want to be ethical leaders make it their way of life to never compromise on certain morals and principles they choose to live by. They communicate the value of ethics articulately and by their actions as well. They coach others to practice ethics in the workplace and to remain true to some principles.

Reinforce Ethical Behaviour: Ethical leaders ensure that to create an ethical environment in the workplace, they reinforce ethical behavior. They train others to practice such behavior while establishing clear dos and don'ts with comprehensible consequences. Good and ethical behavior is rewarded, while unethical behavior is punished. A reward can even be a small compliment or some token of appreciation as long as it reinforces positive and desirable behavior.

Make Ethical Decisions: A person aspiring to become an ethical leader will always ensure that the decisions taken by them do not go against their values and beliefs as well as the mission of the organization. They implement only those decisions that meet their criteria of acceptance. This applies to all decision making arenas. Such leaders are conscious of their actions and their community. Such leaders are likely to make environmentally friendly decisions even if that would lead to a dent in the organization's pocket.

Establish Zero Tolerance for Ethical Behavior: Ethical leaders do not entertain any form of ethical violation. They believe in doing the right thing all the time without any exceptions and questions. As a result, they cannot tolerate any unethical behavior or actions that violate the organization's belief system. They hold others to the sea standard of behavior as they hold themselves.

Practice Justice: Ethical leaders are fair and just by nature. They practice the same by building a mutually respectful relationship with their team members and treating everyone the same. They do not discriminate or favor any employee based on gender, religion, nationality, ethnicity, age, or any other unique factor about them. They listen carefully to every viewpoint and perspective. They give it all equal weightage and make rational decisions without letting any prejudices or biases cloud their judgment.

Recruit Ethical Employees: An ethical leader not only ensures that employees in the organization possess values similar to the organization but also ensures they hire ethical individuals. They hire diverse people who no doubt will be trained but at least have similar fundamental or core values that they share with the organization.

The 4-V Model of Ethical Leadership

When it comes to ethical leadership, some key points from the pillars of successful leadership, they are defined in this 4-V model.

Vision: It is no news that in the successful administration of any team, the leader requires a good vision. He/she should have the necessary foresight to judge the impact of his/her decisions and the team's performance on the business. This vision should include some moral policing of the leader and the team to maintain proper ethical leadership.

Values: Every person lives by some values. A person leading a life without morals is like a flower blooming without any colour and fragrance. In a team, the costs of the leader impact the working of the whole team. An ethical leader should take care that he/she is not compromising on anyone's morals and ethics and then lead the team by establishing values that will motivate the whole team and help them get an identity for themselves.

Voice: What is a leader without a say? Hence, an ethical leader should have a clear vision set on the goal and the way to approach it. Also, it is essential to voice this vision out. There should be transparency in the team, and everyone should know each other's thoughts, especially the leader should take the initiative for this.

Virtues: Virtues are the good points and the ethics which cause no harm to others. An ethical leader should be virtuous and should promote others' virtues and morals as well. Also, he/she should verify that his/her actions are being aligned in line with his/her ethics. The leader should take care that his vision, voice, and values are concurrent with each other.

Ethical leadership is of great importance. A good leader is followed, but a moral leader is respected and trusted. You can take the help of the information given above to sharpen your skills in ethical leadership. To be an ethical leader, it would be good if you surround yourself with those who comprise a sound level of integrity and moral conduct. It will empower you in ethical decision making as well. In the ethical dilemma situations, it would be good for you to take some time for deliberating the most right, constructive, and productive course of action as a whole.

CHAPTER FOUR

Business Etiquette

Business Etiquette is a set of social, professional and cultural sensibilities that a person is expected to possess in order to be considered a well-informed business-person with proper business acumen. Business Etiquette focuses primarily on being polite in your interactions with people and paying them respect while dealing with them, the way you would expect them to. This politeness and respect is not limited to meetings held in person only. In fact, these levels of mutual respect and the polite way of addressing people and dealing with them is extended to business emails, telephonic conversations and business letters too.

Business Etiquette serves as an important tool to bridge gaps and develop a fast network of business-people who have a positive impression of your inter-personal skills and cultural sensitivity. However, it should be kept in mind that Business Etiquette varies from place to place. A set of etiquettes that may be held in high regard in one country might not necessarily be observed closely in another country, and in fact, could be viewed as strange or rude at times.

Significance: Most people mistake Business Etiquette as only a study of cultural differences and the ways in which inter-cultural barriers can be broken. However, the truth of the matter is that multiple cultures and their studies are only a part of Business Etiquette. Corporate culture has a distinct culture. It may not be necessarily an intercultural working place, and yet, there are many unwritten rules and codes of appropriateness that exist and are skillfully followed. These norms are practiced and followed both, between and within companies. For example, employees drawing appreciation from their clients for choosing to dress up in formal wear at a meeting, even if there is no strict dress code. An interesting thing to note is that someone's understanding of Business Etiquette could also be influenced and sometimes even limited by many factors that are prevalent at his working place. Things like a company's mission statement, product lines, image, perception, brand value, reach, business partners, investors, clients and customers can all influence the idea and importance of etiquette in the minds of the company's employees.

First Impression: We create an impression about a person within few seconds of meeting him. This sense of judging a person without knowing anything about him is an in-built quality.

This ability to form an impression of a person, quickly, so that we could categorize him in the friend category helps us to prepare ourselves for self-defense. It activates fight-or-flight defense mechanism, which we act accordingly. In modern terms, this intuition has been given the term first impression. We always tend to respect our gut feeling and listen to our inner voice more than any rational explanation and this forms a foundational quality in all human beings. That's the reason, experts suggest that when you meet someone for the first time, we should strive to achieve the perfect look and present the perfect image. Knowing etiquettes will not only enable us to understand the other person's sensibilities but will also help us present an impression of a gentleman or a woman. It will assist in putting your best foot forward so that the focus of the ensuing discussion will be more on the business topics rather than you looking out of place.

Important qualities

Punctuality: A person on time is a dependable person. This is a general impression punctual people manage to effectively leave on the minds of many people. Someone who appreciates the value of his time will not appreciate waiting for others and others waiting for him.

Preparedness: A person should always be well informed and prepared to furnish information, in detail, on any topic related to his job and responsibility at any given time. This creates an impression of being a resourceful person.

Courteous: You need to be courteous to all the people you are interacting with, instead of limiting the courtesy to only those who you think deserve it. When you are working in an organization that has many talented and creative people in it, there is always a chance that ideas will clash with one another. In that case, you need to tackle the opposing thought and not the person.

Proper Representation of Thoughts: There are times when your thought would be very clear on a particular topic but the choice of your words could send a mixed signal to the listeners. Many people end up being misquoted and misunderstood, due to lack of connection with the people listening to you. You should prepare your presentation thoroughly, beforehand and have a clear understanding of each word and the different ways it can be interpreted. Step in to clear any misconceptions people might have on a point.

Participation: Companies, expect a lot from you. These expectations could be in the form of specific targets, which the company sets for you. In such times, it is very easy to turn your back to a discussion that does not concern you and say – "that's not my problem". However, that problem could well be your problem in the near future. So, try to participate in the problem-solving process.

Properly Dressed: The way you look when you meet someone for the first time goes a long way in establishing a perception of you in that person's mind. That does not mean that you should splurge on the clothes you are supposed to wear. Your clothes should not draw too much attention towards themselves. Dress conservatively but professionally.

Grooming

Business dress code is often a question of common sense prevailing while deciding what to wear to the work place. However, cases of dressing disasters continue to occur, especially during the summers when you might find a colleague dressed up to work with a day at the beach hangover. The reason these eyebrow-raising errors in dress codes occur is that many companies, especially start-ups and small to medium-scale businesses, have relaxed norms to almost no norms on dress code. Even if there are dress code rules, at times, they are vague and ambiguous. In such situations, it is always advisable to err on the part of too formal attire, as opposed to arriving dressed up informally enough to raise a few eyebrows.

Common errors people make in business dressing are –

- **Ill-Fitting Clothes** – Clothes too big give you a bloated look and too tight fitting clothes accentuates the body in a non-formal way. In a meeting, you would not want the attention to shift from you and your presentation towards your clothes.
- **Wearing Short Skirts/Sleeves** – Short skirts and sleeves draw attention to your legs and hands when you sit down. That diverts the attention of the listeners and appears unprofessional.
- **Wearing Short Socks** – Short socks, or drooping socks expose skin and that distracts attention while crossing legs or sitting down. Always

go for socks that cover 3/4th the distance from the ankle to the knee. Avoid wearing white socks as they immediately draw notice towards themselves.

- **Low-Cut or Plunging Tops** – Just as with short skirts, this distracts an interviewer and looks very out of place in a professional environment that requires a conservative dress code.
- **Improper Color Choices** – Colors, like green, yellow, red, etc., do not go down well in corporate circles. They not only draw attention towards themselves but also look unprofessional.
- **Clothes with Quotes, Pictures or Designs** – This lends a very informal and non-serious look to the interviewee. There is always a risk of people associating the slogans and mottos on the t-shirts to be your personal points of view.
- **Poorly-Maintained Shoes** – Shoes are a very important part of your business attire. Shoes, in a way, announce your arrival even before you interact with someone, so naturally, it draws a lot of attention. It is for this reason that your shoes should be always clean and polished.
- **Not Dressing Formally For Business Social Events** – Even dinners at the boss' house are formal business occasions. So, dress accordingly. The general rule about informal business dressing is that it should be treated as formal clothing.
- **Improper Grooming** – Unclipped nails, odorous breath and unkempt hair are all red-checks. If you are one of those who perspire profusely, use anti-sweat deodorants. However, keep in mind that the meetings will be mostly in air-conditioned rooms with very less chance of fresh air entering the room. So, wear a perfume or deodorant of a mild fragrance.

Tips for Grooming

- Avoid noisy and squeaky shoes as they will disturb and distract everyone.
- Trousers' side-pockets should not bulge with mobile phones, wallets etc., as it gives a bulky look to your legs.
- All noticeable body-piercing, tattoos should be concealed, as tattoos are since long, associated with rebellious behavior.
- Do not smoke or eat odorous food before interviews. Use breath fresheners.
- Clean your nails and teeth properly.

Business Dining

When we are invited to our boss' birthday party at his place, we can't be dressed up the way we would had it been our best friend's birthday party. There needs to be a change in not only our dressing but also the manner in which we conduct ourselves. In other words, we need to treat an invitee for any social gathering that involves meeting your co-workers just as you would treat a day at the office, the only difference being that, here you have a liberty to discuss family life and other topics that you generally won't get time to talk about in your professional life. Two situations that arise, invoke the need to understand the need for dining etiquette and learn it - one, if you are the host of a get-together and the second one, if you are the guest.

When You are the Host

Choose a restaurant that is conducive to holding sizeable meetings and provides good service. Make sure that you have made all the adequate bookings and seating arrangements. Clarify the billed amount and availability of desired menu before the meeting itself.

- Arrive fifteen minutes early on the day of the meeting and introduce people to one another if some of them have not been introduced to each other earlier. Offer the seat with the best view to your most important guest.
- While ordering food, try to recommend, what is the best of all the dishes there are on the menu if someone is undecided on what to choose. If that is too direct an approach, then you could help him out in a different way by letting him know what you are ordering, so that he takes the hint.
- Always be done with the ordering, before you start to discuss business with someone. Or else there will be many disturbances with the waiter asking you repeatedly for your order. In addition, the guests will be caught in two minds as to order or to listen to your business discussion.
- If the meeting is to celebrate an achievement or to dedicate it to someone, or is a congratulatory party thrown in honor of someone, it is always nice to speak something about it and make a small toast. It is perfectly all right to toast while sitting. Just hold your glass up and when others follow suit, you can say something to the point and end it.
- Be attentive to the needs of everyone around the table and keep an eye out on their preferences, which will help you to decide upon the right place for any future meetings. You might see that your chief guest has a taste for seafood so you might set up your next meeting at a place where

the seafood is good.

- Always try to engage everybody in a conversation and be the facilitator in leading people to participate in the discussion, bring their points of view and experience into play too. This will help people to come out of their initial inhibitions of meeting someone for the first time and will encourage them to be themselves.

When you are the Guest

Always, promptly reply to an invitation. Your answering will help the host in organizing and coordinating the meeting so try to answer as early as possible.

- Always arrive before time and always inform before time, if you are going to be more than five minutes late. Always take the opportunity to ask your host to recommend you on what you should order to break the ice.
- Many times, you will come across a generous host who will ask you to order what you please. Although you have been given a free rein on your choice of dishes, be considerate while ordering and do not take up this opportunity to order something extravagantly expensive. You are more likely to lose ground with the host that way.
- Always order something in the mid-budget range that would not draw attention towards itself and be easy to eat. Do not order runny, messy food as that might soil your clothes. Try to order food that can be easily eaten with cutlery, as opposed to those dishes where you have to use hands to eat.
- The reason is that there could be a chance that someone arrives late at the table, seats himself beside you, and offers you his hand to greet you. In a situation like this, it would be unsightly to see your hands smeared with food.
- Business dining follows almost the same template of etiquette as business dressing in the sense that, you are not supposed to draw attention towards yourself due to your choice of food while dining, just like you were not supposed to draw attention towards yourself with your clothes in a meeting.
- Always remember that a business dinner or lunch is basically, a professional, formal meeting in a restaurant, instead of a room. Carry the same body language that you would carry when you would sit in for a

business discussion with someone. Have a smile on your face but be on your guard.

- As a rule of thumb, the host is the one who steers the conversation from small talk to business discussion, so wait until he hints before discussing business. When invited to someone's home, it's considered improper to turn up empty-handed. You are not expected to gift something expensive- just a jar, or even desserts would be great.

If there comes a scenario where you have arrived at the table and you see many unknown faces, and the host is not around to introduce you to others, take up the initiative and introduce yourself to others, instead of sitting quietly in a corner and pretending others do not exist.

Rules of Writing

Writing is similar to starting an assignment. You need to be well-planned, prepared, focused, committed, and most importantly, passionate towards what you are doing. If you implement all the following points mentioned, the odds of writing well-appreciated text will be in your favor. First of all, let's accept the fact that very few people, almost none can write a document the way they wanted to put it on paper, in the very first attempt. Ideas and memories often come when least expected, and these new ideas keep on changing your document with each subsequent input. Once you have put your ideas on paper, the next step would be to present it in a simple, logical, connected and clear manner.

Researching on any topic is a very critical step before writing. Your sources need to be reliable and widely accepted. Before you identify and develop your topic, you should find the context and background information on your topic.

This can be done by referring to books, articles, journals, news sources, and magazines. People nowadays use video and sound recordings too. The following steps will help you to –

- Note the important and relevant details.
- Evaluate each point against the topic and purpose of your document.
- Record the details of resource and reference (i.e. author, title and publishing).
- Arrange content in a logical order under appropriate headings and sub-headings.

Knowing the audience pulse before you are writing the document will give a lot of support in deciding on the content and approach. In case you are not aware of the audience, you can write keeping in mind the demographic, i.e. the target group for your write-up, as online article writers or bloggers do. Before you begin to write, try to understand always what your reason of writing is. It could be anyone of the following

Providing information	Sending reports
Applying persuasion	Recommendations
Presenting your opinion	A desired action
Proposing Ideas	Reaching an accomplishment

Enter Caption

For example, if your intention is to sell a product or get someone to subscribe to a service you are providing, or are promoting a cause; ask yourself questions like - who are my potential readers? What is the background of my prospective target readership? Where do they live and how old are they? What are their interests and priorities? These questions will set the purpose for your writing.

Email Etiquette

Email is widely used as a form of inexpensive yet highly effective business communication tool. Printouts of emails are rarely taken and soft copies are used because archiving and retrieving emails is easily. The reason of its popularity is the ease of access, which everyone in an organization starting from the CEO to the janitor can use. Emails are an efficient way to communicate information in a well-presented, easy to read and professionally appropriate manner. Many people quote lack of time as a reason to forward sub-standard emails that range from incomplete to incomprehensible.

Many people mistake emails with text messaging, or at least their approach towards writing emails suggests so. Let us discuss the difference between a text conversation and writing email. In a text message conversation, two people can exchange information, share details, provide corrections and ask for clarifications in a rapid back-forth manner of communication. Compared to this, emails are read by professionals who, depending on their work, may get anything between 20 to 200 emails a day. They neither want to engage in a back-and-forth conversation, nor have the time to ask for details, multiple times. They just want to understand the content of the email, read out the instructions, process the information, get the task done and empty the "unread" section of the inbox.

Risks of Emails

Emails are the preferred mode of communication in many workplaces, and this means they carry a lot of information that could be confidential. Many companies train people extensively on how they are supposed to frame their emails and what kind of emails, to whom they are supposed to forward. The security and confidentiality of the information in the emails is the joint responsibility of both the sender and the recipients. Companies have strict guidelines to safeguard their documents and their contents. Let us discuss some of the most commonly followed guidelines to prevent email misuse.

You and your company will be held liable for numerous legal suits if

- You send or forward emails with offensive content.
- You send an attachment that has a virus.
- You forward the sender's email to another person without permission.
- You try to forge others' emails or send emails from others' accounts.
- You try to conceal your identity from the receivers when sending email.
- You copy a message belonging to another person without permission.

Elements of a Formal Email: While most of us send informal emails to friends that might contain grammatical mistakes in them, the same is not true when writing to colleagues, especially when we want to make a good impression, as we have to be more careful and diplomatic this time. Here are some general tips on the right format of an email –

Background – the default white background should be used for all emails. Colored backgrounds, or scroll designs seem to be unprofessional and distracting.

Font – Preferred fonts are Times New Roman or Arial, Font size-12.

Font Color – Font should be navy blue or black only.

Contact Details – Official contact information like name, designation, email id, contact number, company logo and address of correspondence should be mentioned in the signature area. Personal statements are best avoided.

First Name and Surname – they should be mentioned in the same font as used in the body of the email, only two font sizes larger. Cursive fonts for name is not recommended.

Take emails seriously

Emails are part of today's business world. While you should always consider calling instead of emailing, it's not always feasible. If you do need to send an email, make sure you take it seriously and practice proper email etiquette. Take a few minutes to proofread your email for:

Spelling

Grammar

Typos

The email is an extension of you and your business, and once you press send, there's no getting the email back. There are free tools available online, like Grammar that you can install into your web browser directly. These tools aren't perfect, but they'll catch obvious spelling and grammar errors, and offer suggestions on how to correct them. Also make sure that you provide email addresses for employees. It looks much more professional for employees to send company emails from a business address instead of their personal address.

Telephone Etiquette

Telephonic conversations are fast replacing traditional on-venue meetings, due to the logistics and time saved. It is much easier for people to have a conversation over the phone nowadays, as compared to travelling to a distant place to do the same. Although the obvious advantages of a telephonic conversation are many – one being that the person does not have to be physically present during the time of the interview, this could also be one of its distinct disadvantages.

In a face-to-face conversation, 70% of the person's responses are non-verbal and are related to body language. In a telephonic conversation, you have to make up for that 70% with your voice projection, tone and modulation.

Some Important Points on Telephonic Etiquette –

- Speak loud enough to be heard clearly. Keep your mouth close to the mouthpiece. It is advisable to use a hands-free equipment, if possible, so that your hands are free to jot down points. Many people express their points by the use of their hands to emphasize on specific areas of discussion. Using hands-free equipment will also enhance your expressive skills.
- Let the other person do most of the talking, as he will be explaining what he wants to inform you about, for you to understand. Also speaking out of turn could irritate the listener.
- Smile and speak in a conversational manner. Smiling while talking changes the shape of your mouth when you pronounce the words and the listener easily picks up this change in tone.
- Place a notepad, pen, and a copy of the document that is being discussed near you for reference and jotting down important information.
- Try to go to a place that has as less background noise and interference as possible while attending a telephonic interview.
- If you are stuck in a traffic or a noisy place when someone from office calls and asks if it's the right time to talk to you, excuse yourself politely and offer to call back in 5-10 minutes. This will give you time to go to a silent place to prepare your mood and mind for the conversation.
- Turn off Call-waiting and such applications that give beeping notifications during calls, so that the other person's attention is not diverted due to the distracting sound.

Business Etiquette is one of the most important and yet, most neglected part of a professional's life. If you are not aware of the basic rules of etiquette while meeting new people and dealing with clients, then you are most likely to make many errors that might be unknown or seemingly innocent to you, but could be easily misconstrued as deliberate and offensive by the person listening to you. This was a small step in making you aware of what the simple rules in etiquette that you are expected to be aware of and follow them when you are interacting with people. We hope you are now ready to utilize what you have learnt from this reading and are going to implement that in your life.

CHAPTER FIVE

Change Management

Certain organizations follow a culture where all the employees irrespective of their designations have to step into the office on time. Such a culture encourages the employees to be punctual which eventually benefits them in the long run. It is the culture of the organization which makes the individuals a successful professional.

Every employee is clear with his roles and responsibilities and strives hard to accomplish the tasks within the desired time frame as per the set guidelines. Implementation of policies is never a problem in organizations where people follow a set culture. The new employees also try their level best to understand the work culture and make the organization a better place to work.

The work culture promotes healthy relationship amongst the employees. No one treats work as a burden and moulds himself according to the culture.

It is the culture of the organization which extracts the best out of each team member. In a culture where management is very particular about the reporting system, the employees however busy they are would send their reports by end of the day. No one has to force anyone to work. The culture develops a habit in the individuals which makes them successful at the workplace.

Change management is the discipline that guides how we prepare, equip and support individuals to successfully adopt change in order to drive organizational success and outcomes.

While all changes are unique and all individuals are unique, decades of research shows there are actions we can take to influence people in their individual transitions. Change management provides a structured approach for supporting the individuals in your organization to move from their own current states to their own future states.

INDIVIDUAL CHANGE MANAGEMENT

While it is the natural psychological and physiological reaction of humans to resist change, we are actually quite resilient creatures. When supported through times of change, we can be wonderfully adaptive and successful.

Individual change management requires understanding how people experience change and what they need to change successfully. It also requires knowing what will help people make a successful transition: what messages do people need to hear when and from whom, when the optimal time to teach someone a new skill is, how to coach people to demonstrate new behaviors, and what makes changes "stick" in someone's work. Individual change management draws on disciplines like psychology and neuroscience to apply actionable frameworks to individual change.

ORGANIZATIONAL/INITIATIVE CHANGE MANAGEMENT

While change happens at the individual level, it is often impossible for a project team to manage change on a person-by-person basis. Organizational or initiative change management provides us with the steps and actions to take at the project level to support the hundreds or thousands of individuals who are impacted by a project.

Organizational change management involves first identifying the groups and people who will need to change as the result of the project, and in what ways they will need to change. Organizational change management then involves creating a customized plan for ensuring impacted employees receive the awareness, leadership, coaching, and training they need in order to change successfully. Driving successful individual transitions should be the central focus of the activities in organizational change management.

Organizational change management is complementary to your project management. Project management ensures your project's solution is designed, developed and delivered, while change management ensures your project's solution is effectively embraced, adopted and used.

ENTERPRISE CHANGE MANAGEMENT CAPABILITY

Enterprise change management is an organizational core competency that provides competitive differentiation and the ability to effectively adapt to the ever-changing world. An enterprise change management capability means effective change management is embedded into your organization's roles, structures, processes, projects and leadership competencies. Change management processes are consistently and effectively applied to initiatives, leaders have the skills to guide their teams through change, and employees know what to ask for in order to be successful.

The end result of an enterprise change management capability is that individuals embrace change more quickly and effectively, and organizations are able to respond quickly to market changes, embrace strategic initiatives, and adopt new technology more quickly and with less productivity impact. This capability does not happen by chance, however, and requires a strategic approach to embed change management across an organization.

COMMUNICATION IN CHANGE MANAGEMENT

You cannot over-communicate when you are asking your organization to change. Every successful executive, who has led a successful change management effort, expresses the need for over communicating during a change experience and makes this statement in retrospect. No organization exists in which employees are completely happy with communication. Communication is one of the toughest issues in organizations. It is an area that is most frequently complained about by employees during organizational change and during daily operations. The reason? Effective communication requires four components that are interworking perfectly to create shared meaning, a favourite definition of communication.

· The individual sending the message must present the message clearly and in detail, and radiate integrity and authenticity.

· The person receiving the message must decide to listen, ask questions for clarity, and trust the sender of the message.

· The delivery method chosen must suit the circumstances and the needs of both the sender and the receiver.

· The content of the message has to resonate and connect, on some level, with the already-held beliefs of the receiver. It must contain the information that the employee wants to hear. It must answer the employee's most cherished and cared about questions.

· With all of this going on in a communication, it's a wonder that organizations ever do it well.

Change management practitioners have provided a broad range of suggestions about how to communicate well during any organizational changes.

Communication for Effective Change Management

Develop a written communication plan to ensure that all of the following occur within your change management process.

· Communicate consistently, frequently, and through multiple channels, including speaking, writing, video, training, focus groups, bulletin boards, Intranets, and more about the change.

· Communicate all that is known about the changes, as quickly as the information is available. (Make clear that your bias is toward instant communication, so some of the details may change at a later date.) Tell people that your other choice is to hold all communication until you are positive about the decisions, goals, and progress. This is disastrous in effective change management.

· Provide significant amounts of time for people to ask questions, request clarification, and provide input. If you have been part of a scenario in which a leader presented changes, on overhead transparencies, to a large group, and then fled, you know what bad news this is for change integration. People must feel involved in the change. Involvement creates commitment—nothing else is as significant during a change process.

·Clearly communicate the vision, the mission, and the objectives of the change management effort. Help people to understand how these changes will affect them personally. (If you don't help with this process, people will make up their own stories, usually more negative than the truth.)

· Recognize that true communication is a conversation. It is two-way and real discussion must result. It cannot be just a presentation.

· The change leaders or sponsors need to spend time conversing one-on-one or in small groups with the people who are expected to make the changes.

· Communicate the reasons for the changes in such a way that people understand the context, the purpose, and the need. Practitioners have called this: "building a memorable, conceptual framework," and "creating a theoretical framework to underpin the change."

· Provide answers to questions only if you know the answer. Leaders destroy their credibility when they provide incorrect information or appear to stumble or back-peddle when providing an answer. It is much better to say you don't know, and that you will try to find out.

· Leaders need to listen. Avoid defensiveness, excuse-making, and answers that are given too quickly. Act with thoughtfulness.

· Make leaders and change sponsors available, daily when possible, to mingle with others in the workplace.

· Hold interactive workshops and forums in which all employees can explore the changes together, while learning more. Use training as a form of interactive communication and as an opportunity for people to safely explore new behaviors and ideas about change and change management. All levels of the organization must participate in the same sessions.

· Communication should be proactive. If the rumor mill is already in action, the organization has waited too long to communicate.

· Provide opportunities for people to network with each other, both formally and informally, to share ideas about change and change management.

· Publicly review the measurements that are in place to chart progress in the change management and change efforts.

· Publicize rewards and recognition for positive approaches and accomplishments in the changes and change management. Celebrate each small win publicly

RESISTANCE TO CHANGE

Resistance is a natural response to change and recognizing and managing resistance is a key skill for the effective change manager. Resistance is a healthy part of any change process. Manage it effectively and it can strengthen your change initiative. Ignore it and it can quietly undermine all your great intentions.

Managing resistance to change

Recognise resistance: Don't pretend it's not happening - it will not go away, but will quietly fester and grow to be much bigger than it really is. It is most important first of all to recognise and acknowledge the resistance.

Don't shoot the messenger: Just because someone has spoken out, don't assume they are the only one resisting - there may be many more quietly agreeing with them.

Open it up for discussion: Often easier said than done but if you recognise resistance, then ask questions and find out about it. Listen to what people say and don't think about whether you agree or disagree with them.

Understand their concerns: Try to understand what might be really worrying them. Does your plan have some real weaknesses? Could their concerns have some basis? Are they worried about their own capacity or skills? Whilst they might not want to admit it, is it possible that they feel they don't have the ability or knowledge necessary? Or are they going to lose status? Or control?

Give it some time: Allow time for the concerns to be raised and then work with your team to find shared solutions

Motivation and resistance to change

Key to managing resistance is understanding motivation. For each member of your team think about what their motivation might be, how this will be affected by the change and how you might revise your change plans accordingly.

Organizational Learning

Learning is the way we create new knowledge and improve ourselves. Although there is ample debate regarding the mechanisms and scope of learning, in its simplest form this is no different for organizations. Botha et al. describe the organizational learning process as follows

CHAPTER SIX

Conflict Resolution

What is Conflict: For some, the definition of conflict may involve war, military fight, or political dispute. For others, conflict involves a disagreement that arises when two or more people or parties pursue a common goal. Conflict means different things to different people, making it very difficult to come up with a universal or true definition. To complicate this even further, when one party may feel that they are in a conflict situation, the other party may think that they are just in a simple discussion about differing opinions. To fully understand conflict and how to manage it, we first need to establish a definition that will allow us to effectively discuss conflict management and its use by today's leaders. Conflict can be described as a disagreement among two entities that may be portrayed by antagonism or hostility. This is usually fueled by the opposition of one party to another to reach an objective that is different from the other, even though both parties are working towards a common goal. To help us better understand what conflict is, we need to analyze its possible sources. According to American psychologist Daniel Katz, conflict may arise from 3 different sources: economic, value, and power.

- **Economic Conflict** involves competing motives to attain scarce resources. This type of conflict typically occurs when behavior and emotions of each party are aimed at increasing their own gain. Each party involved may come into conflict as a result of them trying to attain the most of these resources. An example of this is when union and management conflict on how to divide and distribute company funds.
- **Value Conflict** involves incompatibility in the ways of life. This type of conflict includes the different preferences and ideologies that people may have as their principles. This type of conflict is very difficult to resolve because the differences are belief-based and not fact-based. An

example of this is demonstrated in international war in which each side asserts its own set of beliefs.

- **Power Conflict** occurs when each party tries to exert and maintain its maximum influence in the relationship and social setting. For one party to have influence over the other, one party must be stronger (in terms of influence) than the other. This will result in a power struggle that may end in winning, losing, or a deadlock with continuous tension between both parties. This type of conflict may occur between individuals, groups, or nations. This conflict will come into play when one party chooses to take a power approach to the relationship. The key word here is "chooses." The power conflict is a choice that is made by one party to exert its influence on the other. It is also important to note that power may enter all types of conflict since the parties are trying to control each other.

Conflict can occur in various ways in the human experience, whether it is within one-self between differing ideas or between people. Even though this chapter will focus on the conflict at the social level, it is important that we review all the different levels of conflict that may exist. The levels of conflict that we will discuss include interpersonal, intrapersonal, intergroup, and intragroup conflict.

Levels of Conflict

- **Interpersonal Conflict.** This level of conflict occurs when two individuals have differing goals or approaches in their relationship. Each individual has their own type of personality, and because of this, there will always be differences in choices and opinions. Compromise is necessary for managing this type of conflict and can eventually help lead to personal growth and developing relationships with others. If interpersonal conflict is not addressed, it can become destructive to the point where a mediator (leader) may be needed.
- **Intrapersonal Conflict.** This level of conflict occurs within an individual and takes place within the person's mind. This is a physiological type of conflict that can involve thoughts and emotions, desires, values, and principles. This type of conflict can be difficult to resolve if the individual has trouble interpreting their own inner battles. It may lead to symptoms that can become physically apparent, such as anxiety, restlessness, or even depression. This level of conflict can create other

levels of conflict if the individual is unable to come to a resolution on their own. An individual who is unable to come to terms on their own inner conflicts may allow this to affect their relationships with other individuals and therefore create interpersonal conflict. Typically, it is best for an individual dealing with intrapersonal conflict to communicate with others who may help them resolve their conflict and help relieve them of the situation.

- **Intergroup Conflict.** This level of conflict occurs when two different groups or teams within the same organization have a disagreement. This may be a result of competition for resources, differences in goals or interests, or even threats to group identity. This type of conflict can be very destructive and escalate very quickly if not resolved effectively. This can ultimately lead to high costs for the organization. On the other hand, intergroup conflict can lead to remarkable progress towards a positive outcome for the organization if it is managed appropriately.

- **Intragroup Conflict.** This level of conflict can occur between two individuals who are within the same group or team. Similar to interpersonal conflict, disagreements between team members typically are a result of different personalities. Within a team, conflict can be very beneficial as it can lead to progress to accomplishing team objectives and goals. However, if intragroup conflict is not managed correctly, it can disrupt the harmony of the entire team and result in slowed productivity.

Regardless of the level of conflict that takes place, there are several methods that can be employed to help manage conflicts. And with the seemingly infinite triggers for conflict, management of conflict is a constant challenge for leaders. To help address this, we will next discuss what conflict management is and then later examine the role of leadership in conflict management and resolution.

Five Conflict-Handling Modes (Avoiding, Accommodating, Competing, Collaborating, and Compromising)

Avoiding: This mode is low assertiveness and low cooperative. The leader withdraws from the conflict, and therefore no one wins. They do not pursue their own concerns nor the concerns of others. The leader may deal with the conflict in a passive attitude in hopes that the situation just "resolves itself." In many cases, avoiding conflict may be effective and beneficial, but on the other hand, it prevents the matter from being resolved and can lead to larger issues. Situations when this mode is useful include:

when emotions are elevated and everyone involved needs time to calm down so that productive discussions can take place, the issue is of low importance, the team is able to resolve the conflict without participation from leadership, there are more important matters that need to be addressed, and the benefit of avoiding the conflict outweighs the benefit of addressing it. This mode should not be used when the conflict needs to be resolved in a timely manner and when the reason for ignoring the conflict is just that.

Accommodating: This mode is low assertiveness and high cooperation. The leader ignores their own concerns in order to fulfill the concerns of others. They are willing to sacrifice their own needs to "keep the peace" within the team. Therefore, the leader loses and the other person or party wins. This mode can be effective, as it can yield an immediate solution to the issue but may also reveal the leader as a "doormat" who will accommodate to anyone who causes conflict. Situations when this mode is useful include: when an individual realizes they are wrong and accepts a better solution, when the issue is more important to the other person or party which can be seen as a good gesture and builds social credits for future use, when damage may result if the leader continues to push their own agenda, when a leader wants to allow the team to develop and learn from their own mistakes, and when harmony needs to be maintained to avoid trouble within the team. This mode should not be used when the outcome is critical to the success of the team and when safety is an absolute necessity to the resolution of the conflict.

Competing: This mode is high assertiveness and low cooperation. The leader fulfills their own concerns at the expense of others. The leader uses any appropriate power they have to win the conflict. This is a powerful and effective conflict-handling mode and can be appropriate and necessary in certain situations. The misuse of this mode can lead to new conflict; therefore, leaders who use this conflict-handling mode need to be mindful of this possibility so that they are able to reach a productive resolution. Situations when this mode is useful include: an immediate decision is needed, an outcome is critical and cannot be compromised, strong leadership needs to be demonstrated, unpopular actions are needed, when company or organizational welfare is at stake, and when self-interests need to be protected. This mode should be avoided when: relationships are strained and may lead to retaliation, the outcome is not very important to the leader, it may result in weakened support and commitment from followers, and when the leader is not very knowledgeable of the situation.

Collaborating: This mode is high assertiveness and high cooperation. In this mode both individuals and teams win the conflict. The leader works with the team to ensure that a resolution is met that fulfills both of their concerns. This mode will require a lot of time, energy and resources to identify the underlying needs of each party. This mode is often described as "putting an idea on top of an idea on top of an idea" to help develop the best resolution to a conflict that will satisfy all parties involved. The best resolution in this mode is typically a solution to the conflict that would not have been produced by a single individual. Many leaders encourage collaboration because not only can it lead to positive outcomes, but more importantly it can result in stronger team structure and creativity. Situations when this mode is useful include: the concerns of parties involved are too important to be compromised, to identify and resolve feelings that have been interfering with team dynamics, improve team structure and commitment, to merge ideas from individuals with different viewpoints on a situation, and when the objective is to learn. This mode should be avoided in situations where time, energy and resources are limited, a quick and vital decision needs to be made, and the conflict itself is not worth the time and effort

Compromising: This mode is moderate assertiveness and moderate cooperative. It is often described as "giving up more than one would want" to allow for each individual to have their concerns partially fulfilled. This can be viewed as a situation where neither person wins or losses, but rather as an acceptable solution that is reached by either splitting the difference between the two positions, trading concerns, or seeking a middle ground. Leaders who use this conflict-handling mode may be able to produce acceptable outcomes but may put themselves in a situation where team members will take advantage of the them. This can be a result of the team knowing that their leader will compromise during negotiations. Compromising can also lead to a less optimal outcome because less effort is needed to use this mode. Situations when this mode is effective include: a temporary and/or quick decision to a complex issue is needed, the welfare of the organization will benefit from the compromise of both parties, both parties are of equal power and rank, when other modes of conflict-handling are not working, and when the goals are moderately important and not worth the time and effort. This mode should be avoided when partial satisfaction of each party's concerns may lead to propagation of the issue or when a leader recognizes that their team is taking advantage of their compromising style

Leaders should be capable of using all five conflict-handling modes and should not limit themselves to using only one mode during times of conflict. Leaders must be able to adapt to different conflict situations and recognize which type of conflict-handling mode is best to employ given the conflict at hand. The use of these modes can result in positive or negative resolutions and it is imperative that today's leaders understand how to effectively employ them

Leadership and Conflict Management

The leader's role in managing conflict can have a significant impact on how they are resolved within the workplace or organization. Leaders spend about 24% of their time resolving conflicts, however the process to approaching conflict management relates to a great extent to their leadership style. Leaders who use conflict management skills can provide guidance and direction towards conflict resolution. A common trait of leaders is they are able to build teams that work well together and help to set the tone for the organization. They must be able to facilitate the resolution of conflicts through effective conflict. Leaders exhibit a variety of characteristics and traits that allow them to be great leaders, but does it help them when it comes to conflict management? I believe that it does. These same traits can help leaders dealt with conflict. The ability to recognize one's own leadership style will ultimately help describe how a leader handles conflict. It is up to the leader to assess what action, if any, is needed and then intervene with the specific leadership function to meet the demand of the situation. To be an effective leader, one needs to respond with the action that is required of the situation. I feel this demonstrates that the job of a leader is to analyze a conflict and facilitate the situation to produce a resolution that can be positive and productive.

Leadership skills needed to be effective at conflict management can be categorized to show which skills match up with five of the conflict-handling modes. The avoiding mode requires leadership skills such as: to be able to withdraw from a conflict or sidestep issues, have the ability to leave issues unresolved, and to have a sense of timing. The accommodating mode requires skills such as: being able to obey orders, set your own concerns aside, selflessness, and the ability to yield for the greater good. The competing mode requires skills such as: standing your ground, debating, using influence, stating your position clearly, and stressing your feelings.

The collaborating mode requires skills such as: active listening, identifying concerns, analyzing input, and confrontation. The compromising mode requires skills such as: negotiating and finding the middle ground, making concessions, and assessing value.

Behaviors that allow leaders to be effective at conflict management include:

- **Be Candid.** Leaders cannot hesitate to put issues on the table to be discussed
- **Be Receptive.** Leaders need to make sure that team members understand that it is ok for conflict to exist and that everyone's opinion will be discussed
- **Depersonalize.** Leaders must be able to remove personal feeling from the mix and view conflict as a team issue
- **Learn to Listen.** Leaders must listen carefully and make sure that they provide feedback as well
- **Be clear.** Leaders need to make sure that all team members understand how decisions will be made to resolve the conflict
- **Out-law Triangulation.** Leaders must prevent team members from "ganging-up" on others that they may disagree with
- **Be Accountable.** Leaders must make sure that they follow through on their actions but also hold others to their actions as well
- **Recognize and Reward.** Leaders must be able to recognize successful conflict management and then reward it

Effective leaders know how to bring conflict situations out into the open so that all parties involved can begin to work towards a resolution that will benefit everyone. They manage conflicts in way that it is seen as an opportunity to build productive relationships

Conflict management must be a part of a leader's toolbox and be deployed when conflict arises within a team or organization. If conflict is not addressed in a timely manner, it can not only affect the moral of the team/organization but can create larger issues later. Once this happens it may be more difficult to resolve then it would have been if the conflict was addressed immediately and effectively. Leaders must be able to recognize that conflict can cause negative issues within their team or organization. If they are able to pull on their leadership skills and recognize which conflict-handling mode is required for each situation, they can create an opportunity to improve team structure and dynamics, and ultimately achieve their goal of changing, developing, and transforming organizations.

CHAPTER SEVEN

Customer Service

Many businesses rely on quality customer service to attract and retain customers. Giving employees the tools to provide the highest quality service possible is the goal of any customer service manager. Starting with smart recruiting to providing structured feedback, managers can improve on customer service leadership qualities. Customer service team success is most significantly influenced by service-focused culture that starts at the top and works its way throughout the company. In today's highly competitive marketplace, the most popular businesses attribute a large part of their success to having a customer service mindset that has the power to build a strong brand image and product differentiation. To develop and cultivate that mindset, every company needs to put effort into refined hiring process, constant employee training and growing leaders who will set the tone for other team members to follow.

The role of leadership in customer service should be one of ensuring that it is an on-going and relentless activity that gets ingrained completely in the fabric of the organization. We all know that in the daily tasks of customer service teams, there are several times when customers complain or express their irritation about the company, its offerings, and the service. The managers and team leaders, often would keep this 'information' from the top leaders, not just to save themselves from the ire of top leadership but also may be because the culture of the company dictates that the top leadership must be 'protected' from such 'bad news. It is essential that these barriers are removed. There must be an active role of top leadership in customer service such that they can help fix some of the more daunting challenges the teams may face. There can be no shortcuts to service excellence and an active role of leadership in customer service would ensure that everyone in the company understands this and does their bit to enhance consistently the standards of service. The other advantage of having the involvement of leadership in customer service is that employees have someone to emulate and there is a heightened sense of belonging and ownership, making it easier to care genuinely for the customer. Customer service is a challenging realm of business as it is and hence consistently enhancing service levels to meet customer demands would be a herculean task for any company. This is where an active role of leadership in customer service is required – to ensure that the company lives and breathes customer service and is constantly geared towards service excellence. Without effective leadership, attaining this to keep pace with customer demands would be impossible. A company cannot achieve top levels of service by hanging service quotes on the office walls or any other such surface level actions. The role of leadership in customer service would ensure that a service culture is embedded firmly into the organization and in everyone working there. The role leaders of the company would essay in making customer service a success, would be to help the teams address any tough issues and secondly to emphasize and reiterate the importance of positive customer experiences. Of course, leaders need to allow room for the employees to do their job and do not require to 'spoon feed' them in the daily tasks. Leaders must display openness and honesty such that employees remain encouraged to speak to them and share their concerns in a spirit of trust. The role of leadership in customer service is therefore manifold – one of the main tasks would be to inspire trust and dependability in both external and internal customers. By treating the company's employees well and being there when they need their leaders, would encourage the employees to pass on this positivity to the external customers, thereby raising the trust quotient and reputation of the company.

The task of the leaders of a company is not easy. While employees could be allowed outbursts occasionally, leaders need to conduct themselves with discipline and ensure their behaviour is exemplary. If they want employees to let them in on the truth at all times, leaders must have a reputation of listening patiently and making fair decisions. The role of leadership in customer service then would be to help their employees to respond and act logically even in the face of crisis and demanding customers. For the success of any organization, the role of leadership in customer service must go beyond advice – it must be participative. It would be highly recommended that leaders mingle with the front-line staff, and be part of the service to get a first-hand experience of the kind of service the company provides and how customers view it. Leaders must step out of their 'abodes' and move around with the employees on the office floor – this would give the employees a sense of being cared for and would make them more engaged. Employees must be empowered to make spot decisions for customers – this not only makes customers happier, but also saves huge amounts of time and energy for the company. Some autonomy to employees makes them feel trusted and valued – they would in turn, take the initiative to pass on these feelings when serving customers. This is the indirect role of leadership in customer service. Employees look up to their leaders and tend to follow any behaviour they exhibit – it is therefore extremely vital that leaders display model behaviour at all times. Their behaviour – both good and bad, would most definitely pass on to customers through the service employees impart.

We now know that customer service is the responsibility of everyone in an organization and this begins with the role of leadership in this realm. Simply providing lip service to this important and crucial aspect of the company does not suffice leaders must show how to serve customers through example and begin with internal customers. Leaders of a company cannot ask their employees to work with high standards and serve customers at all times, unless they do so themselves. The role of leadership in customer service and in every other realm is to understand their employees and the customers first, before they expect others to do so. The leaders of a company must be able to create cohesion and a sense of purpose for the employees – they should be able to communicate a clear vision of the company and the role of customer service in achieving that vision. The role of leadership in customer service would also be to communicate effectively, solve problems, and manage conflict such that the workforce is able to deliver on their tasks stress-free and with enthusiasm. However, the leaders treat the employees, would be the way employees treat the external customers. Hence, even if leaders may not directly deal with external customers regularly, what they do with the workforce would directly affect the quality of customer service the company provides.

Clear Goals: A customer service leader should spend time reviewing the job description of each service employee. The job description is the foundation of expectations for an employee. Using the job description as the starting point, a customer service leader can clearly communicate what the baseline expectations are for each employee and build on higher quality standards.

Involve Employees: No one likes to be judged yet it is imperative to evaluate employee performance. One way to reduce the strain of employee evaluations is to involve each employee in the process. Provide everyone with a self-evaluation form that has each employee review his own strengths and weaknesses. Good employees have honest self-perceptions and are more willing to take criticism and training in areas of weakness. Of course, it is imperative to note all strengths as well to let the employees know what is being done well. Let employees know how you rate yourself and your personal goals for improvement. This puts everyone on track to performing at a higher standard.

Understand Every Job: A service manager that doesn't understand everything required in an employee's position runs the risk of giving job demands that don't fit the scenario. A manager who can perform the employee's job is better able to empathize and recognize structural issues that affect customer service performance. For example, a hotel manager who is complaining that his valet's are not bringing cars up faster can see that the service elevator is the culprit, not the employees, if he spends a day on the line. This information allows the manager to take proper action to rectify the problem rather than constantly berate employees for slow service.

Empower Employees: Allow employees to provide feedback and suggestions about goals and issues affecting goal achievement. Conduct meetings and training sessions that not only help service representative improve within their position but also provides opportunities for growth and promotion. Don't be afraid to explain to employees the reasoning behind doing something a specific way or why learning something outside the job description may be helpful. Sometimes an establishment may provide a service in a way that takes too long and seems archaic, but if employees are told that the reason is a long-standing tradition, employees can take pride in the history of what they do. Doing so makes them a part of the history and may increase service performance.

Build a Customer Centric Structure and Culture

The uniquely cross-functional nature of effective customer-experience efforts puts a premium on smart governance. Adequately addressing the challenge requires a dedicated effort on three levels. First, a customer centric leadership structure must ultimately report to the chief executive and should be designed to stimulate cross-silo activity and collaboration. Second, leaders must commit to demonstrating behaviors and serving as role models to deliver customer-experience goals to frontline workers and refine and reinforce those goals over the long term. Finally, it is necessary to put in place the correct metrics and incentives that are critical for aligning typically siloed units into effective cross-functional teams. Contact center leaders cited poor cross-departmental collaboration and lack of understanding and respect for the center as two of the top three challenges they're currently dealing with.

Businesses tend to rate the customer experience their company delivers higher than consumers do. Despite the attention to customer experience that is widely stated in corporate missions, visions, and values, actions speak louder than vision statements. When it comes to resources and budget, CEOs tend to prioritize technology over people or process. Even when company leaders recognize that customer service could be better, they often will look to the latest technology to provide the solution without delving deeper into customers' true wants and needs, or gathering insights from frontline staff. Leaders have a huge impact on building a customer centric culture. The leader must be customer obsessed and share those values and goals with the company employees. Does the leader walk the talk? Does the leader put customers first? Are products, services, and processes created with customer needs and wants shaping results? If the company is focused on short-term results or is investing in areas that do not improve the customer experience, employees will pick up on this and leaders will get behaviour from employees that are not customer focused. Leaders who want to deliver exceptional customer experiences need to invest in employee incentives that will steer performance toward exceptional service.

Time-Sensitive Customer Service Training

Sometimes, customer service training can't be planned. Perhaps there's a product recall, a major rebranding, or a national advertising campaign. Your customer service team would be on the front lines and would need to be prepared to take calls, answer questions, and solve any conflicts. Customer service training, in this case, would be all about equipping your team with everything they need to know to do their job.

Here's what urgent customer service training might consist of:

- **In times of crisis.** In the event of a recall, crisis, or company emergency, your customer service team should be updated on all events and trained on how they can respond. Full transparency is encouraged here, given that your team will be dealing with the public's response first-hand. Make these trainings a priority on everyone's calendar and try to have

your team trained all at once — this will keep everyone aligned.
- **Product or company updates.** This type of customer service training is less of an emergency but just as time-sensitive. Whether you release a product update, run a major marketing campaign, or alter your website, your customer service team should complete training on these updates and be equipped to handle any customer questions or concerns.

CHAPTER EIGHT

Customer Support

Customer support as the act of providing timely, empathetic help that keeps customers' needs at the forefront of every interaction. Instead of the stereotypical view of customer service as a cost center, customer support teams are the face of the company. They play a critical part in sales and word-of-mouth marketing, work side-by-side with product teams, and have a seat at the table when it comes to company decision making. Modern customer support is a much more all-encompassing role that plays a part in the entire customer lifecycle from acquisition to retention.

In the self-service internet age, customers don't need go-betweens to assist them with what should be simple functions, like canceling their account. Many businesses continue to direct their energies toward protecting revenue by putting these speed bumps in place, but they waste time that could have been spent solving a problem that only a human can solve.

And what's more, people have grown to expect self-service if you let them get to a point where they have to reach out, you've gotten in the way of usage and adoption. Customer-centric companies remove a lot of that friction by automating that which can be automated and freeing their most valuable resource — their team — to work on problems that can't be automated away. Hence the shift away from hiring your average people person, toward hiring highly skilled, empathetic problem-solvers. Even the call centers of yore are making way for contact centers: partners in revenue generation and customer experience, populated with highly educated staff that have career paths and incentives beyond calls-per-minute.

Make sure your team has the right tools: While it's certainly possible to run your entire support operation using a shared Gmail or Outlook mailbox, it's not always the best way to set your team up for success. Dedicated customer service software is often a better choice for enabling your team to deliver excellent support. Tools that have been designed specifically for support teams offer features like shared inboxes, built-in help centers, saved replies, automated workflows, duplicate reply prevention, and customer relationship data. These features help your team deliver personalized, fast, and expert service with every customer interaction.

Offer self-service support options: Sometimes, delivering excellent customer support means making it easy for customers to help themselves. In fact, 81% of consumers attempt to resolve issues on their own before reaching out to customer support, and 71% want the ability to solve most issues on their own. Make sure you have a knowledge base that includes answers to frequently asked questions and how-to articles that walk customers through the steps required to solve common problems. Next, make it easy for customers to find that documentation by optimizing your content for search (both within your knowledge base and on the major search engines), structuring your knowledge base logically, or adopting a tool like Help Scout's Beacon that surfaces relevant content when customers initiate live chat.

Hire for key support skills: Some of the most important skills for support professionals are patience, attentiveness, the ability to communicate clearly, a willingness to learn, and empathy. Your team needs to be composed of people who want to learn everything there is to know about your product because they genuinely want to help your customers succeed. They must be willing to dig in to troubleshoot issues, solve problems outside of their domain, and actively listen to customers to determine what they really need. To attract skilled professionals, you'll have to pay rates that are attractive to skilled professionals, and you'll need to offer career advancement opportunities that are far more varied than simply moving into a team management role.

Give your team authority to use their skills: Having to check with management to solve all but the most basic requests will disempower even the most competent agents. In addition to being skilled enough to answer complex questions, they must also be empowered to solve requests on their own. For example, INR 1,000 rule: Everyone on your customer service team can spend up to INR 1,000 per guest, per incident to resolve guest issues. But empowering your team doesn't have to be quite so extravagant; it can also be as simple as documenting policies and guidelines in a place that's easy for everyone on your team to access. The guidelines you document don't even have to be specific. Use creative (and where possible, inexpensive) methods to delight customers encouraged employees to come up with and share lots of inexpensive solutions to customer problems.

Foster effective problem solving: The call center customer service teams of the late 20th century were held to operational metrics tied to cost-cutting, such as first response times and call resolution times. But providing excellent customer support means focusing more on holistic metrics that are tied to company-wide goals, such as customer satisfaction and NPS. Solving requests in a reasonable time frame is still important. But great customer service beats speed every time. Customers understand that more complex queries take time to resolve. There's a difference between the time it takes you to respond and the speed at which you resolve their problems. They'll spend as much time as it takes to resolve their issues. Encourage your team to get back to customers in a timely fashion, but don't hold them to metrics that make them feel rushed to close requests before a customer's issues are completely resolved.

Make it easy for customers to get support: If you search Google for "(company) customer support," in most cases Google populates a featured snippet containing the contact information for that company. There's a reason for that: Some companies bury their contact information to make it difficult for customers to get in touch when they have problems. Don't make your customers turn to Google to find out how they can get in touch with your support team. Make it easy for them by displaying your contact information in logical places on your website. Also, consider meeting them where they are by offering live chat support within your product or accepting support requests over social media.

Don't prioritize automation over personalized support: Automation is a great addition to your team's toolkit because, when used correctly, it eliminates some of the mindless, repetitive tasks that keep your support agents from delivering attentive, personalized service. And in some cases, AI tools are even great for customers because they provide quick, instant answers to simple questions. But when used incorrectly, chatbots can easily become the voice-activated phone menus of the online customer support age. They misunderstand questions, pointing customers to the wrong resources, or send customers around in circles trying to solve problems that require critical thinking and other exclusively human skills. While customers like quick, easy answers, they expect more human service when it comes to solving complex problems. They don't want to be referred to as a ticket number, don't want to repeatedly provide long explanations as they're transferred to different teams, and don't appreciate generic responses to genuine concerns. Make sure that the tools you use make it easy for your team to see who they're speaking to before they respond — and that those tools don't get in the way of your ability to provide personalized, human support when it's needed.

CHAPTER NINE

Cyber Security

Cyber security leadership and management are two high-level competences required to successfully administer a cyber security division that produces the essential level of security, trust and stability (STS) demanded by an organization. Although leadership and management are prerequisite expertise for all information systems security officers (ISSO) and/or chief information security officers (CISO), they must always be intentionally cultivated. Using industry standards, frameworks and models as guidance, this learning path will focus on the key objective elements (KOE) by discussing the information security strategies' alignment with the organizational strategy, regulatory systems and operational excellence.

Types of cyber threats

Common cyber threats include:

- **Malware**, such as ransom ware, botnet software, RATs (remote access Trojans), rootkits and boot kits, spyware, Trojans, viruses, and worms.
- **Backdoors**, which allow remote access.
- **Form jacking**, which inserts malicious code into online forms.
- **Crypto jacking**, which installs illicit crypto currency mining software.
- **DDoS (distributed denial-of-service) attacks**, which flood servers, systems, and networks with traffic to knock them offline.
- **DNS (domain name system) poisoning attacks**, which compromise the DNS to redirect traffic to malicious sites.

Company must make efforts to boost cyber security through following way:

1. Organizations must leverage public-private partnerships and build upon existing initiatives and resource commitments. Through partnership

with government, the IT industry has provided leadership, resources, innovation, and stewardship in every aspect of cyber security since many years. Cyber security efforts are most effectual when leveraging and building upon these existing initiatives, investments, and partnerships.

2. Organizations reflect the borderless, interconnected, and global nature of today's cyber environment. Cyberspace is international and unified system that spans geographic borders and traverses national jurisdictions. Countries should exercise leadership to encourage the use of bottom-up, industry-led, globally accepted standards, best practices, and assurance programs to promote security and interoperability

3. Firms must be able to adapt rapidly to emerging threats, technologies, and business models and be based on effective risk management. Efforts to improve cyber security must be based on risk management. Security is a means to realize and make sure continued trust in various technologies that comprise the cyber infrastructure. Cyber security efforts must help an organization's ability to appropriately understand, assess, and take steps to manage ongoing risks in this environment.

4. Efforts to improve cyber security must focus on awareness. The principle of cyber security is to focus on raising public awareness. Cyberspace's owners include consumers, businesses, governments, and infrastructure owners and operators. Cyber security efforts must help these stakeholders to be attentive of the risks to their property, reputations, operations, and sometimes businesses, and better understand their important role in helping to address these risks.

5. Efforts to improve cyber security must more directly focus on bad actors and their threats. The unified, global, and digital nature of the cyber infrastructure also has presented cyber criminals with completely new crime opportunities. Security practices serve to counter these opportunities and allow cyber-based transactions and activities to occur.

6. In cyberspace, as in the physical world, adversaries use instruments to do crime, spying, or warfare. Cyber security policies must allow governments to better use current laws, efforts, and information sharing practices to respond to cyber actors, threats, and incidents domestically and internationally

Reasons for Commission of Cyber Crimes

There are many reasons which act as a catalyst in the growth of cybercrime. Some of the prominent reasons are:

a. Money: People are motivated towards committing cybercrime is to make quick and easy money.

b. Revenge: Some people try to take revenge with other person/ organization/society/caste or religion by defaming its reputation or bringing economical or physical loss.

This comes under the category of cyber terrorism.

c. Fun: The amateur do cybercrime for fun. They just want to test the latest tool they have encountered.

d. Recognition: It is considered to be pride if someone hack the highly secured networks like defense sites or networks.

e. Anonymity- Many time the anonymity that a cyber space provide motivates the person to commit cybercrime as it is much easy to commit a cybercrime over the cyber space and remain anonymous as compared to real world.

It is much easier to get away with criminal activity in a cyber-world than in the real world. There is a strong sense of anonymity than can draw otherwise respectable citizens to abandon their ethics in pursuit personal gain.

f. Cyber Espionage: At times the government itself is involved in cyber trespassing to keep eye on other person/network/country. The reason could be politically, economically socially motivated.

Ways to Improve Cyber Security

Cyberspace is a worldwide and interrelated sphere that covers geographic borders and national jurisdictions. To support the growth, operation, maintenance, and security of this area, information technology companies continually innovate and spend in the development of internationally deployable products and services. Cyberspace's stakeholders such as consumers, businesses, governments, and infrastructure owners and operators, search for a consistent, secure experience in cyberspace. Efforts to improve cyber security should mirror cyberspace's borderless nature and be based on internationally established standards, best practices, and international assurance programs. This approach will augment security, because nationally focused efforts may not have the advantage of the best peer-review processes conventionally found in global standards bodies, because proven and effectual security measures must be deployed across the whole global digital infrastructure, and because the need to meet multiple, conflicting security requirements in multiple jurisdictions raises enterprises' costs, demanding valuable security resources. Cyber security standards also improve interoperability of the digital infrastructure, because security practices and technologies can be better united across borders. It also allow more private-sector resources to be used for investment and innovation to address future security challenges and increase international trade in cyber security products and services that can be sold in multiple markets.

Cyber security is need of organization in technologically advanced business climate. In a situation of global connection and cyber terrorism, the security of information assets is vital to all private business, public organization and individual household. With the expansion of the internet as a global infrastructure for business and as a new device for politics, espionage and military activities, cyber security has become central theme for national and international security. The objective of a cyber-security management system is to shield the confidentiality, integrity and availability of information assets. Two appropriate cyber security management system technologies are effective that include perimeter defence and encryption. These concepts and solutions are consistent and joined together in practical application. A thoroughly conceived and consistently rendered cyber security management policy facilitates to move the application of these technologies forward. The concepts of policy and technology are basic to an effectual cyber security management system. Good cyber security can maintain privacy in an electronic environment, but information that is shared to assist in cyber security efforts might sometimes include personal information that at least some observers would regard as private. Cyber security is an effectual way of protecting against undesired observation and gathering of intelligence from an information system.

CHAPTER TEN

Delivering Constructive Criticism

There is a right way and a wrong way to deliver constructive criticism, especially in the workplace. Take the right approach, and all parties involved will benefit. Take the wrong approach, however, and the entire situation could take a turn for the worse. One of the primary responsibilities of people management is to help employees reach their peak potential. This often means providing criticism, even when it's difficult to do so. The key to constructive criticism is getting your point across without talking down to the other party. It sounds simple, but it takes a targeted approach to ensure you don't cross the line.

Constructive criticism in the workplace is a form of actionable feedback focused on improving some aspect of employee performance. It can play an essential role in a company's overall performance management process. When done correctly, constructive criticism is conveyed in a positive manner with the good intention of employee improvement. It is not the act of attacking or tearing someone down for poor performance. Whenever you're offering constructive criticism, it's critical to come prepared with clear and specific examples of what the employee needs to improve, as well as possible solutions and next steps for performance improvement. That way, you aren't simply complaining about the employee's work, but providing them opportunities to grow and make things right.

Constructive criticism vs. destructive criticism

The big difference between constructive and destructive criticism lies in how the comments are delivered. While constructive criticism focuses on building up the other person, destructive criticism focuses on the negative. The feedback can be vague and often lacks guidance or support.

Constructive criticism: Constructive criticism is clear, direct, honest, and easy to implement. It provides specific examples and actionable suggestions for positive change. This type of feedback also highlights ways the recipient can make positive improvements in their behavior to minimize future problems.

Deconstructive criticism: Destructive criticism, on the other hand, focuses solely on the problem. This kind of feedback offers no encouragement, help, or support for improvement. Despite the deliverer's intentions, it often lowers morale and reduces confidence.

Benefits of constructive criticism

Unlike deconstructive or negative criticism, constructive criticism builds trust and provides an opportunity for both parties to grow. Two key elements of constructive criticism's success are context and actionable advice. This kind of feedback gives the recipient context around their areas of improvement, which is crucial for understanding why the feedback is being offered. Supporting the additional context with actionable steps and suggestions for how to improve build trust between both parties. This combination also opens the door to conversation, collaboration, and professional development.

How to offer effective constructive criticism

When the time comes to deliver constructive criticism, following these steps can help ensure your criticism is well received.

1. Schedule a time for private feedback: No one likes to be surprised by constructive criticism, especially not in front of other people. Such instances are a surefire way to put the employee on the defense, which is not ideal for receiving feedback. To ensure the employee is in the right headspace to accept constructive criticism, schedule a time to meet with them, and be honest about the topic. Briefly explaining what you want to talk about beforehand will allow them time to prepare mentally and physically. Since you don't want to surprise or embarrass the employee, it's important that your meeting is conducted somewhere private. Regardless of how well-intended you are, offering constructive feedback will not achieve your desired result if your whole team is listening in. Keeping your feedback private will allow you and the employee to have an open and honest conversation without anyone else interfering.

2. Focus on actions, not personality traits: When you focus solely on the person, your constructive criticism can be misconstrued as a personal attack on their character. This is another way you may inadvertently make the person become defensive. Instead, focus on specific actions that need to be addressed so that they are receptive to change. For example, let's say an employee is repeatedly turning in assignments with the same error. Instead of attacking their character by saying they're lazy or incompetent, you could teach them the proper way to fix the error and then suggest that double-checking their assignments before submitting them would help improve their work and reduce the amount of time spent on corrections afterward. By pointing out the benefits of changing their actions, you are turning a negative into a positive. It shows the person that while they need to make a change, doing so could work in their favor.

3. Be specific: When you're specific with your constructive criticism, down to the finest of details, there is no gray area. The other person knows exactly what you are saying. But if you're vague with your feedback, it can be challenging to get your point across, and your criticism won't have the intended effect. Consider this scenario: An employee keeps forgetting to use the CRM software that the rest of the team uses, which has resulted in cross-function problems. Vague feedback could sound something like, Sanju, don't forget to check out the CRM software if you get a chance." That doesn't convey that there is an ongoing issue and doesn't let Sanju know why he needs to use the CRM software. A leader needs to be specific about what the problem is, what they want the employee to do and how this action will benefit them. Specific feedback for this instance could sound something like, Sanju, please take the time to properly implement the CRM software that the rest of the team is using. I am sure it will help you achieve even greater results. This advice is direct, to the point and almost a command. In contrast, the vague example is nothing more than a half-hearted attempt at guidance, with the outside hope that the person will listen.

4. Provide ideas and resources for improvement: Giving constructive criticism without offering ideas for improvement can often come across as a personal slam and make a manager appear unhelpful. This may not be your intention, but it could be the end result if there's no context or guidance given. If you're going to provide feedback, make sure you're ready to follow it up with actionable advice on how the employee can improve. For example, if an employee gave a terrible presentation that lacked important information, instead of simply telling them that the presentation missed the mark because it didn't have the necessary statistics, you could say something like, overall, the presentation was solid, but in the future, please provide more data and statistics around our sales numbers. You can find plenty of information by scouring our monthly sales reports, speaking with Kathy and reading our most recent newsletter. With this approach, you're clear in your criticism about the presentation but also providing detailed information that can result in immediate improvement. If you want the employee to improve, you need to point them in the right direction. This is the "constructive" part of "constructive criticism.

5. Create a supportive environment of continuous feedback: Foster a supportive workplace that engages in both formal and informal feedback in the form of an open dialogue. A supportive environment and nurturing tone can improve an employee's receptiveness to constructive criticism. For example, instead of using negative language, keep it positive and encouraging. Focus on how the changes you're suggesting can benefit the employee and the company. Emphasize that you always want to ensure the employee is set up for success by regularly discussing any issues that arise. Also make sure the conversation is always a two-way street. Give the employee time to ask questions and offer their perspective on things. This not only helps them feel valued, but it can also clear up any confusion on expectations and gain their buy-in.

Before you dive in and begin to provide feedback, you must set your objectives. What are you trying to accomplish? What results will you be happy with? No two situations are the same, but these strategies can keep you on track:

- In a positive manner, make the person aware that they need to work on something in particular.
- Don't just provide criticism; provide solutions to the problem.
- Take the necessary steps to decrease the likelihood of the same issue occurring in the future.

For example, if you have a salesperson who has difficulty being organized, here is what you can do to deliver constructive criticism successfully:

- Schedule a meeting to address the problem, noting the benefits associated with staying organized at all times.
- Get "hands on" to ensure the person is aware of the best solution, such as implementing the use of CRM software and other organizational tools

helpful in sales.

- Provide actionable steps for avoiding the same trouble in the future. In this case, you can give the employee a detailed checklist for staying organized.

It is one thing to set objectives. It is another thing entirely to have a plan for providing constructive feedback based on those objectives.

The benefits of constructive criticism in the workplace

When constructive criticism is delivered the right way, it can serve many benefits for you and your employees.

- **It improves employee performance.** Leaders who fostered supportive environments for feedback had much better performance improvements than those operating in unsupportive environments. When criticism is given constructively in a supportive climate, employees are more open to accepting it and can improve their performance by acting on the feedback in a timely manner
- **It fosters creativity and brainstorming.** A workplace that expects and thrives on constructive feedback is primed for growth and innovation. A study on cooperative criticism found that "the optimal context for creativity in brainstorming is a cooperative one in which criticism occurs but is interpreted constructively because the brainstorming parties perceive their goals as aligned." Encouraging the employee to set and track these goals can also keep them motivated and on task.
- **It enhances collaboration.** Creating an environment where employees and managers feel confident engaging in open feedback and constructive criticism can be a great way to improve collaboration. Instead of feeling as though they are being attacked for poor behavior and are on their own, employees are more likely to receive constructive criticism well if they are invited to work with someone on improvements. Peer mentoring, career coaching and group projects are all ways employees and leaders can help one another become better at their respective jobs.

How to receive criticism with tact and grace:

1. Stop your first reaction. Stay calm and try not to react at all. Maintain a calm demeanor.

2. **Remember the benefits of getting feedback** and try to understand the motivation and perception of your criticizer.

3. Be a good listener. Listen closely and focus on understanding the other person's comments and perspective.

4. **Say thank you.** You don't have to agree with the feedback, but expressing gratitude demonstrates that you recognize the efforts of your colleagues who are working towards your improvement.

5. **Ask questions** to deconstruct the feedback and share your perspective. Get more clarity by asking for specific examples, acknowledging the non-disputable part of the feedback, and asking for concrete solutions.

If you are on the receiving end of constructive criticism, don't throw it away. Insight from a trusted, objective source about your work, management style, or how you're showing up is priceless. You want to keep it coming, and that means not reacting in a way that scares the giver off or makes them less willing to give you feedback in the future.

To keep the feedback coming, avoid these 5 reactions:

1. Do not react with defensiveness and anger
2. Do not attack the person giving the feedback
3. Do not interrupt or talk over the person when they are giving the feedback
4. Avoid analyzing or questioning the person's assessment initially
5. Avoid engaging in a debate or a combative response

CHAPTER ELEVEN

Developing Corporate Behavior

Every business has a set of values and ethics. Aligning these characteristics with the standards of conduct is what makes a business stand out and be a leader in the business world. Adopting positive leadership behavior can motivate your team to be more effective and increase its ability to reach goals. It also helps you to retain top talent within your department, as team members will value the opportunity to work alongside you. Learning how to behave like a leader can take practice and a strong sense of self-awareness as you monitor your own actions. In this article, we discuss why leadership behaviors are so important within an organization and share some simple steps you can take to start to develop your own effective leadership behavior.

The organization's base rests on management's philosophy, values, vision and goals. This in turn, drives the organizational culture that is composed of the formal organization, informal organization, and the social environment. The culture determines the type of leadership, communication, and group dynamics within the organization. The workers perceive this as the quality of work life which directs their degree of motivation. The final outcome are performance, individual satisfaction, and personal growth and development. All these elements combine to build the model or framework that the organization operates from.

Good leadership behaviors are crucial to become someone who inspires and leads people to maximize efficiency and to achieve the goals of the organization. Leadership behaviors are essential to:

- **Increase the productivity of a team:** Consistent leadership can motivate a team to greater performance.

- **Retain people:** Employees are less likely to leave if they receive great leadership and mentorship in their current roles.
- **Nurture future leaders:** Leadership behaviors are integral to develop and nurture future leaders within an organization.

Historical Development of Organisational Behaviour

The history of human relations is not new. It existed since the beginning of the time but its dealings is quite new with the development of art and science. In the early days people worked alone or in small groups where human relations were not problem because organisations were not as complicated as they are today. Human relations are handled very easily because there were direct links between labour, capital and management. They were supposed to be happy in such conditions in fulfilling their needs Actual conditions were brutal and backbreaking. Life was very hard those days. People worked from dawn to dusk under intolerable conditions of disease, filth, danger and scarcity of resources. They had to work to survive hence there was no possibility of trying to improve the behavioural satisfaction. Then industrial revolution broke in. In the beginning there was no improvement in human relations but later on improvement was seen in the working conditions of the people. The industry generated a surplus capital of goods and knowledge that eventually provided workers increased wages, shorter hours of work and more work satisfaction.

Popularity: During Second World War and after, the industrialists and academicians showed a great interest in human relations in organisations. It was due to short supplies of labour during war period. By the 1950s, the study of the subject because of fashion of the day and it became popular. Main reasons of its popularity were

(i) There was a cultural lag in understanding the human side of organisation so that heavy emphasis was laid on its study to achieve development equivalent to that in engineering, production, sales, etc.

(ii) Mayo and Roethlisberger researches were followed by fresh researches, giving managers new understanding in building up a more effective organisation.

(iii) Labour unions gained strength and pressed for better working conditions for the workers. Workers also were better educated and expected better work environment, and more human quality leadership in organisation. There was a change in social attitudes demanding more social responsibility from organisations.

(iv) Work-environment itself became more complex and needed more attention. Size of organisation increased considerably that multiplied the complexity of work. Increased specialization also contributed to the complexity of work because now workers were unable to understood the whole product.

The reasons discussed above show that the emphasis given to organisation behaviour was a result of trends, development over a long period of time.

Impact of Technology on Organisational Behaviour

Technology is considered as the basic factor in the process of economic development. In organisational environment, technological changes means the technical knowledge used in the production of capital and machinery. The modern changes in technology lead to increase in the productivity of labour, capital and other production factors. Technology as a systematic application of scientific or other organised knowledge to practical tasks. The technology is the powerful means of wresting power from nature in all possible ways. Technology strengthens the faculties of men and enables them to harness gigantic physical forces of nature. Technological change is not a mere improvement in the technical know-how. It means much more than this. It should be preceded by sociological change also, a willingness and desire on the part of community to modify their social, political and administrative institutions so as to make them fit with new techniques of production and faster tempo of economic activity.

TECHNIQUES RELEVANT TO ORGANISATIONAL BEHAVIOUR

1. Re -engineering: Re engineering is the fundamental and radical redesign of business processes to achieve dramatic improvements in critical, contemporary measures of performance such as cost, quality, service and speed. Many TQM approaches are designed to increase efficiency by streamlining current operations. Re engineering however, involves a total redesign of operations by analysing jobs and asking : How can this work be done most efficiently? Rather than modifying current work procedures, the reengineering process begins with a clear state and plans the job from beginning to end. Re-engineering allows the organisation to eliminate inefficiencies and increase productivity.

2. Bench Marking: Benchmarking is the process of company work and service methods, against the best practices and outcomes for the purpose of identifying changes that will result in higher quality output. It incorporates the use of human resources techniques such as goal setting to set targets that are pursued, identified and then used as a basis for future action. The bench marking process involves looking inside and outside the organisation to find ways and means to improve operational efficiency. It is benefitial.to the Organisations because : (a) This technique helps organisations compare themselves against successful companies for the purpose of identifying improvement strategies. (b) It enables organisations to learn for others. (c) It helps create a need for change by showing the organisation how procedures work assignments should be altered and resources reallocated.

3. Empowerment: Empowerment is the authority to make decisions within one's area of operations without having to get approval from anyone else. It has two unique characteristics: (a) The personnel are encouraged to use their initiative. (b) Employees are given not just authority but resources, as well, so that they are able to make a decision and see that it is implemented. There are several basic conditions necessary for empowerment to become embedded in the organisational culture and become operational

(i) Participation : Empowerment assumes that all employees are willing to improve their daily work processes and relationships.

(ii) Innovation : Empowerment encourages innovation because employees have the authority and bring out new ideas and make decision that result in new ways of doing things.

(iii) Access to Information : When employees are given access to information, their willingness to cooperate and use their empowerment is enhanced.

(iv) Accountability : Although employees are empowered to make decisions they believe will be most beneficial to the organisation, they are also held accountable for results. However thus accountability is not intended to punish personnel or to generate immediate short term results. Instead, the intent us to ensure that the empowered employees are giving their best efforts, working towards agreed upon goals, and behaving responsibility towards each other. If these behaviours are exhibited then management continues to empower employees to proceed at their own place in their own way.

The main concern for the managers in any organisation is to persuade people to work together in a coordinated manner and achieve the goals of the organisation. The role of the manager is similar to that of a conductor of an orchestra. Different musicians who are playing their different instruments. And if they are able to work in a coordinated manner they can come out with a beautiful musical composition. And it is primarily the responsibility of the conductor that they are trained to work together in such a coordinated manner. So is the job of the manager.

Models of Organizational Behavior

There are four major models or frameworks that organizations operate out of, Autocratic, Custodial, Supportive, and Collegial

Autocratic—The basis of this model is power with a managerial orientation of authority. The employees in turn are oriented towards obedience and dependence on the boss. The employee need that is met is subsistence. The performance result is minimal.

Custodial — The basis of this model is economic resources with a managerial orientation of money. The employees in turn, are oriented towards security, benefits, and dependence on the organization. The employee need that is met is security. The performance result is passive cooperation.

Supportive — The basis of this model is leadership with a managerial orientation of support. The employees in turn are oriented towards job performance and participation. The employee need that is met is status and recognition. The performance result is awakened drives.

Collegial — The basis of this model is partnership with a managerial orientation of teamwork. The employees in turn are oriented towards responsible behavior and self-discipline. The employee need that is met is self-actualization. The performance result is moderate enthusiasm.

Although there are four separate models, almost no organization operates exclusively in one. There will usually be a predominate one, with one or more areas over-lapping with the other models.

The first model, autocratic, has its roots in the industrial revolution. The managers of this type of organization operate mostly out of McGregor's Theory X. The next three models build on McGregor's Theory Y. They have each evolved over a period of time and there is no one best model. In addition, the collegial model should not be thought as the last or best model, but the beginning of a new model or paradigm.

McGregor's Theory X and Theory Y

Douglas McGregor (1957) developed a philosophical view of humankind with his Theory X and Theory Y — two opposing perceptions about how people view human behavior at work and organizational life. McGregor felt that organizations and their managers followed one or the other approach:

Theory X

People have an inherent dislike for work and will avoid it whenever possible.

People must be coerced, controlled, directed, or threatened with punishment in order to get them to achieve the organizational objectives.

People prefer to be directed, do not want responsibility, and have little or no ambition.

People seek security above all else.

In an organization with Theory X assumptions, management's role is to coerce and control employees.

Theory Y

Work is as natural as play and rest.

People will exercise self-direction if they are committed to the objectives (they are NOT lazy).

Commitment to objectives is a function of the rewards associated with their achievement.

People learn to accept and seek responsibility.

Creativity, ingenuity, and imagination are widely distributed among the population. People are capable of using these abilities to solve an organizational problem.

People have potential.

In an organization with Theory Y assumptions, management's role is to develop the potential in employees and help them to release that potential towards common goals.

Theory X is the view that traditional management has taken towards the workforce. Most organizations are now taking the enlightened view of theory Y (even though they might not be very good at it). A boss can be viewed as taking the theory X approach, while a leader takes the theory Y approach.

Key skills of organizational behavior

1. **Identify and promote positive behaviors:** "Prosocial" behaviors within an organization are those which benefit other individuals and the company as a whole. Leaders at every level of the organization need to be able to identify, promote and reward these behaviors -- and conversely, to discourage behaviors that lead to mistrust and other poor interpersonal dynamics between people who must work together.

2. **Create a positive workplace culture:** Individual "prosocial" behaviors do not necessarily occur naturally. New hires do not come into

organizations with a mental makeup optimized for the success of their companies. They must first be incentivized, in part through rewards, recognition, perks and bonuses. The right incentives are the building blocks of a supportive and selfless workplace culture.

3. **Motivate employees to exhibit "prosocial" behaviors:** This discipline offers a set of motivational tools for managers to use, which takes into account individual differences between employees. Effectively, this skill is applied psychology and sociology for managers.

4. **Identify the causes of "antisocial" behaviors:** Toxic behaviors that can infect a department and spread throughout an organization may originate with individuals; they may come from the top down; or they may even be the result of external or internal influences. A manager with expertise in organizational behavior will be able to find the root causes of negative behaviors and develop plans to solve the identified problems.

5. **Assess likely employee response before initiating organizational change:** Predictive capabilities are among the most important for managers, and become even more important as leaders work their way up in the organizational structure. In order to determine the right strategies and implement them successfully, leaders at every level must be able to accurately anticipate how employees will react, and work to develop contingencies. The study of organizational behavior enables this predictive capability.

The importance of studying organizational behavior

At its core, organizational behavior analyzes the effect of social and environmental factors that affect the way employees or teams work. The way people interact, communicate, and collaborate is key to an organization's success. By analyzing and understanding these parameters, you can leverage organizational behavior to improve the effectiveness and efficiency of your workforce. It can also help you achieve the following organizational and work culture goals.

Better communication channels and protocols: Individual employees respond differently to various methods of communication and behave in certain ways due to the structure of the workplace and the organization's culture, values, and goals. They tend to align better with teammates and managers who mirror their behavioral strengths. As such, a keen grasp of organizational behavior can enable middle management to build more effective teams and communicate better with frontline employees.

Leveraging insights from studying organizational behavior can help you understand whether your employees respond better to an autocratic or a supportive model of management. This ensures that you have a firm grasp of the policies, communication channels, and incentives that will best enable your employees to perform well.

Comfortable work environment: One of the key benefits of organizational behavioral analysis is the creation of a suitable workplace environment for employees. With many employees now working from home, it's important for business leaders to create a positive and empowering work setting to facilitate seamless team communication and collaboration. As such, the study of organizational behavior is essential for businesses looking to adapt to the disruptions and challenges resulting from things like the pandemic or shifts in market forces.

Influencing management style: Savvy businesses use data to drive decision-making around the formation of their corporate structure. Having management looking over employees' shoulders at every turn indicates distrust, engenders micromanagement, and leads to negative workplace culture. By observing this trend through organizational behavioral analysis, many enterprises are adopting a flatter, more linear (rather than hierarchical) structure to provide employees with more freedom over how they perform their tasks or whom they collaborate with. Such a structure recognizes the unique differences among employees and enables employees to have a greater voice and contribute to decisions that affect them, their teams, and the larger organization. It also enables business leaders to build a stronger relationship rooted in communication, trust, and transparency with their employees.

Building a winning people strategy: Employees want to work for organizations with a positive culture and an appealing work environment. They also want to get along with other employees and management while working to achieve the organization's goals and objectives. The challenge is creating a workplace that fosters trust, open communication, and seamless collaboration while simultaneously catering to the unique needs of individual employees or certain functions. Creating a winning people strategy requires business leaders to define how they interact with and nurture the development of employees and work culture. It is very much a relationship-focused effort, and organizational behavior is the facilitating linchpin.

Influencing human resource strategies: Business leaders can increase the value of their human capital by studying the complex nature of employees and their interrelationships with others. The insights that such a study provides can help drive human resources reforms and strategies, particularly with recent findings showing a collapse of work-life balance (due to more employees working from home). HR personnel can identify struggling groups needing more support and apply motivational tools (uniquely suited to the employees) to help them perform better by improving their workplace experience.

Conflict resolution: Proactive business leaders nip problems in the bud before they develop into full-scale confrontations. Measuring organizational behavior can help with preventive conflict resolution by identifying where and why your employees are having issues with fellow teammates and management. Behavioral dynamics can help you understand the cause of a problem, predict its course, and head off potential consequences before the issue escalates.

The core concept behind organizational behavior is the certainty that a happy and productive workforce results in a successful organization. Drawing heavily on behavioral/social sciences and psychology, organizational behavior takes a human-centric approach to facilitating a performance-oriented workforce. As such, a deep understanding of organizational behavior and why it's important can help busin

CHAPTER TWELVE

Handling a Difficult Customer

Facing a difficult customer, whether in person, on the telephone or via direct messaging, email or social media, is many people's worst nightmare. If talking to customers is part of your role, however, it is almost inevitable that you will have to deal with a difficult customer sooner or later. Learning how to manage those conversations will be a useful skill for the future. Difficult customers are not just encountered when they make a complaint, although this is often the case. Sometimes, though, the most difficult customers to satisfy are those who have contacted the company for the first time, because you have no history with them, and therefore have less information about how to treat them. For those customers, it is doubly important to listen carefully to what they are telling you, because that will give you important information.

It's important to effectively deal with difficult customers because proper customer service can help you retain customers. It's a great way of turning a negative situation into a positive one, and can encourage the customer to become an advocate of your brand or product because of how well you handled their situation and frustrations. Difficult customers may walk away feeling more impressed after your interaction, as opposed to an ordinary customer who may not have had as much interaction with you.

The importance of customer satisfaction

Establishing and maintaining a good relationship with your customers is key to the success of your business. Although "the customer is always right," they may not always be easy to deal with. Learning how to respond to difficult customers is an important step for any business owner, especially those who work in the customer service industry. Even businesses with the best products and services are bound to have occasional run-ins with angry customers. To build a positive reputation with consumers, it is important to have properly trained staff who can handle difficult people and resolve customer complaints. The first strategy in turning an unhappy customer from grumpy to grateful is to thank them for sharing their bad experience with you. Our natural response is to get defensive and get into a negative mindset with a disgruntled client, Once you flip the switch and start with 'thank you,' the response is out of the ordinary for them. This works in every business, and once the strategy is taught to the customer service teams, sales divisions and leadership, the impact is amazing. However, handling a difficult customer doesn't stop there. The following section will cover several other scenario-specific techniques and strategies that your team can learn to enhance the quality of customer service when dealing with different types of challenging customers.

Types of difficult customers you may encounter

The following are some difficult customers that you may encounter:

- Angry
- Indecisive
- Demanding
- Critical

Angry: Angry customers can be especially challenging. A good first step is to apologize, even if you don't feel like you have done something wrong. This simple action can help to calm them down so that you can move on to a more productive conversation. An angry customer may raise their voice, but you should keep your voice at a normal level. You may even want to soften your voice. The most important part of handling an angry customer is to remain calm and never reciprocate their anger.

Here are examples of what you could say to an angry customer:

- "I really want to help. Thank you for bearing with me as I troubleshoot this for you."
- "I apologize that you received the wrong product, and I understand how inconvenient and frustrating that can be. Please know that we are working on sending a replacement overnight."

Indecisive: Indecisive customers can take a long time to make decisions and may ask many questions. One way you can help them is by determining their specific concerns regarding the purchase. You can reassure them by speaking confidently about the product or service and sharing as much useful information with them as you can. Indecisive customers will help you to practice patience.

Here are a few ways you can handle an indecisive customer:

- Ask them specific questions to help identify their concerns.
- Offer suggestions and explain where, how and why they can use the product or service so that the customer has a chance to imagine themselves benefitting from the product or service.

Demanding: Demanding customers may have a misunderstanding of how you are able to help them. A demanding customer may ask you to do something that you are not authorized or otherwise able to do for them. With this type of customer, you can assure them that you will do whatever you possibly can to meet their needs. And be prepared to compromise if they are asking for too much.

Here are examples of what you could say to a demanding customer:

- "I'm sorry to say that I cannot refund you 100 in cash, but I can refund you 50 in cash and issue you 50 in store credit. Would that work?"
- "Unfortunately, I'm unable to fulfill this request, but let me bring in my manager who may be able to help more."

Critical: A critical customer may find fault in your services, products or something else regarding your business. They may be quick to point out their dissatisfaction. To manage this customer, listen to them patiently and understand their point of view. Sometimes, these customers offer great feedback through their honesty.

Here are examples of what you could say to a critical customer:

- "Honestly, that is such a great suggestion, thank you! I'm going to submit that to our engineering department so they can consider it."
- "I understand that this product line may not be for everyone, and I appreciate your honesty.

Dealing With Different Type of Customers

Though there are many types of difficult customers, the following are some strategies you can use to maintain excellent customer service when dealing with difficult customers:

1. Keep your communication professional: When you're communicating with the customer, keep your language professional, friendly and respectful. Your behavior reflects your employer or business, and it is always good to be mindful of your actions and repress any impulses to take the difficult customer's behavior personally. To manage professional communications, keep an even tone and positive demeanor that shows your customer that you're open to the feedback they're giving. For example, you could make eye contact and/or use their name when responding. A customer's behavior is complex, and you will likely not understand all the factors that influence their decisions. Remaining objective and professional will help you to maintain a service-oriented demeanor.

2. Remain calm and collected: Take a deep breath and tune into your emotions when you're interacting with difficult customers. It is in your best interest to relax and make every customer interaction as smooth as possible. When you stay calm, you keep the situation from escalating into more difficult communication. Practice mindfulness when you are interacting with customers. Ask yourself, "How are they making me feel right now?" You may notice that your heart is racing or you are not breathing deeply. Notice the tension in your body and make a conscious decision to keep the present situation from stressing you out. Your interaction with the customer is more likely to be successful if you learn how to recognize and modulate your emotions. For example, if a customer is angry, you may choose to maintain a helpful yet serious tone.

3. Speak softly: In a situation where a customer raises their voice, it may be best to speak even more softly than normal. You may want to approach them calmly and speak quietly and slowly. A calm presence helps to keep the situation under control and manageable. Speaking softly is a strategy that may be useful for de-escalating tense conversations.

4. Practice active listening: Active listening is a skill that improves comprehension and communication in conversations. It involves focusing your intention on the speaker, understanding what they are saying and responding in a thoughtful manner. Active listening helps you to understand the significance of the customer's words so that you can do your best to make the situation better. So you may need to use active listening when your customer needs reassurance that you're engaged in the conversation. Giving the customer your undivided attention should seem respectful, and it will help you to fully understand the problem and how to come up with solutions. One way to practice active listening is to use verbal affirmations that let the speaker know you are listening and engaged in the conversation. The following are some examples of verbal affirmations:

- "I understand."
- "Yes, I agree."
- "I know what you mean."
- "I hear you."
- "That makes sense."

Active listening is a skill that takes practice to master. It is important in the workplace because it helps you to identify and solve problems effectively.

5. Give them time to talk: People want to be understood. Show the customer that you are listening to them. Nod your head and give them ample time to express themselves before you respond. Giving them time to express their minds will help you to understand the situation and give the customer time to work out their thoughts and feelings. It can be tempting to talk over them, but you should wait until there is a natural lapse in the conversation.

If the situation allows, let the customer know that you want to hear their words and you'll remain silent so you can absorb all they are saying without interrupting.

6. Understand the customer's point of view: When managing difficult customers, you can take time to reflect on their point of view. Empathy skills help with understanding another person's feelings or intentions. Practicing empathy allows you to understand the present emotional state of the customer and respond accordingly. It takes two people to participate in an interaction. In the case when you're speaking with a customer, the customer may need to express their frustration, and you want to hear them out so you can help. If you want to better understand a customer's point of view, try asking questions. Clarifying their needs can help them to know your genuine desire to make it right and allow them to relax knowing you want to help.

To practice empathy, try to:

- Nod.
- Ask the customer what their ideal solution is.
- Be respectful.

- Take responsibility by using phrases such as, "You're right, we did that wrong."

7. Assess their needs: One of the best ways to deliver customer service is to figure out the specific needs of each customer. Taking the time to understand the needs of the customer will help you resolve their issues more quickly. Let the customer know that you will do everything in your power to address their complaint.

8. Seek a solution: Sometimes, it can be useful to simply ask the customer what they need. For example, you could say, "What do I need to do to make this better for you?" This can help you get straight to satisfactory solutions, and focusing on solutions will give you a better chance of resolving the situation quickly. This option is best when you're not sure which actions would ease a customer's mind. Allow them to name their ideal solution so you have a better chance of meeting their expectations and/or finding a compromise and retaining them as a customer.

9. Ask for support: In some cases, you may need to ask for support from another coworker or manager. Calling on support can help you in some situations to solve a customer's problem or answer their questions. Let a customer know that you are bringing someone else into the conversation who may have a better perspective or has more authority to solve their problem. For example, you may want to bring a manager into the conversation if a customer is demanding more than you're qualified to give for the inconvenience. Sometimes customers appreciate this extra step as it reassures them that their concerns are being heard by someone who can make larger decisions on how to move forward.

10. Maintain a positive relationship: When you are finished helping a client, make sure to ask them if there are any other concerns. They might have been so focused on the original problem that they forgot another issue. This also lets the customer know that you still respect and appreciate having them as a customer. If the customer has been inconvenienced, you may consider offering them a gift card or credit, if it's within your authority to do so.

CHAPTER THIRTEEN

Networking Within the Company

Networking is what we do every day when we talk, text, email and meet new people with the purpose of sharing information. While external networking helps us grow our connections to professionals outside of our organization, networking with coworkers helps us grow and strengthen connections with professionals inside our organization – with the added benefit of increasing productivity and engagement internally. Internal networking is something many of us do naturally every day. Like external networking, internal networking is about building a group of people who know you and will help you if they can.

Networking is the process of gathering, collecting and distributing information for the mutual benefit of you and the people in your network. You are not selling, you are telling. You are not asking for flavours, you are giving valuable information, help or support. Networking - creating a fabric of personal contacts who will provide support, feedback, insight, resources and information. Leadership networking is about building relationships and making alliances in service of others - customers, clients, constituents, peers, bosses, and employees - and in service of the organisation's work and goals. A robust leadership network helps provide access to people, information and resources

Although internal networking is talked about less, there are many advantages for both the employee and the organization.

Internal networking promotes:

* development of great ideas
* gathering insights into other functions within a company
* collecting industry information

- learning more about functional roles and open roles
- mentoring and career development
- collaboration between departments

Benefits: For most professionals, external networking is a key way to discover career opportunities in new companies and industries. Internal networking follows the same idea, just internally: By asking the right questions of the right people within your organization, you can grow your career in your company. Engaging in casual conversation with members of your own organization will help you discover useful information (such as which certifications may be beneficial for your professional development), learn about new industry and business trends, generate new project ideas, gain details about upcoming product/service launches, discover company needs that may lead to role opportunities and get a better understanding of the company mission and vision. For organizations, encouraging internal networking leads to lower rates of employee turnover because team members feel connected and tend to have a clearer picture of their organization's purpose. Remember the saying, 'what goes around comes around?' Building mutually beneficial relationships can have a positive impact on individual career satisfaction and on the future of the organization.

How do you do it?

Be strategic. Identify your targets, rate contacts based on level of influence, then prioritize to figure out who to connect with first. Your internal priorities might include:

- people you already know
- people who already interact with your department in some way
- people who may be in a position to help you reach career goals
- people in different areas of the business who might otherwise help you

If you feel awkward about internal networking, you may be wondering where the line is between networking and brownnosing. The answer to that question lies in your mindset, attitude and how well you are able to offer as much as you ask. To begin, proactively plan your actions and make sure you don't cross over the line from making new social connections to bothering people. The key here is to understand how complimenting people just to get in their good graces is not networking. You want to be authentic.

One way to accomplish this is to be an active listener – truly listen to what people are saying and observe their body language and tone. When feedback is provided, it should be reflective with follow-up questions so the other person knows you're engaged. Lastly, be open and honest in your responses.

Research your internal contacts prior to meeting with them to identify how they might be able to help, and ask yourself what you could learn from them that would be valuable. Some questions you may want to ask your targets include:

- Is there any general advice you would give me to be successful in this department?
- Could you tell me about your role here?
- What do you find most rewarding in your role/in the company?
- What are the opportunities in your department?
- Have you taken any good classes, workshops or webinars that I may find interesting?
- Are there opportunities for us to collaborate?
- Is there anyone else in the organization that you think would be good for me to introduce myself to?
- What might I be able to do for you?

Listening carefully and taking notes is also important. People love talking about themselves, so asking them honestly about their experiences can make for more interesting and mutually beneficial conversations, and lead to new learnings and opportunities.

Formal Communication Network – A formal communication network is one which is created by management and described with the help of an organizational chart. An organizational chart specifies the hierarchy and the reporting system in the organization. Therefore, in a formal network, information is passed on only through official channels such as memos, bulletins and intranet (email within the organization).

The organizational chart implies that information can flow in any of three directions – vertically, i.e., upward or downward, and horizontally.

1. Upward Communication – This may be defined as information that flows from subordinates to superiors. Some of the reasons for upward communication include discussing work related problems, giving suggestions for improvement and sharing feelings about the job and coworkers. This type of communication has both benefits and disadvantages. One of the biggest benefits is problem-solving. Once a subordinate has brought a problem to his superior's notice, chances are that the problem will not recur, since the subordinate learns from his superior how to tackle it the next time. Thus, his ability to solve new problems and therefore his managerial ability, improves. Another benefit that could arise from upward communication is that valuable ideas and suggestions may sometimes come from lower level employees. Therefore organizations should encourage this kind of communication. A third benefit is that employees learn to accept the decisions of management and thereby work as a team. The biggest problem associated with this type of communication is that it may lead to "handing down" of decisions by superiors. When subordinates frequently seek the superior's guidance, the latter may adopt an authoritarian approach and merely give instructions, disregarding the subordinate's opinion completely.

2. Downward Communication – This may be defined as information that flows from superiors to subordinates. The most common reasons for downward communication are for giving job instructions, explaining company rules, policies and procedures and giving feedback regarding job performance. A number of studies have indicated that regular downward communication in the form of feedback given to employees is the most important factor affecting job satisfaction. Therefore organizations today are trying to encourage more of this type of communication.

There are both benefits and disadvantages associated with this type of communication. Downward communication that provides regular feedback will be beneficial if the feedback or review of performance is constructive. A constructive review is one where a manager "counsels" an employee, or advises him on how to improve his performance. On the other hand, a destructive review can destroy employee morale and confidence. Regular downward communication also creates a climate of transparency or openness, where information is passed on through official channels, rather than through rumors. Thirdly, downward communication boosts employee morale, since it indicates that management is involved in their progress. The problems with this type of communication are the danger of doing destructive reviews, as mentioned, and that of "message overload." This means that superiors many sometimes burden their subordinates with too many instructions, leading to confusion.

3. Horizontal Communication – This type of communication is also known as "lateral" communication. It may be defined as communication that takes place between co-workers in the same department, or in different departments, with different areas of responsibility. For example, Sales Managers and Advertising Managers in the Marketing department, or Marketing Managers and Finance Managers. The reasons for this type of communication are for coordination of tasks, sharing of information regarding goals of the organization, resolving interpersonal or work related problems and building rapport. The biggest potential benefit of horizontal communication is the sense of teamwork that is created. Regular communication of this type ensures that all co-workers work together towards achieving a common goal in the overall interest of the organization. The biggest potential problem is that conflicts such as ego clashes are bound to arise, when co-workers at the same level communicate on a regular basis.

Internal Networking help the employee: Someone you already know or someone you could meet tomorrow from another department might be the critical linchpin in your success. Building on existing contacts and identifying and cultivating new associations is the key to career growth. It's all about asking questions, offering help and maintaining mutually beneficial and ongoing communication within your network. You never know what jobs are coming down the pipeline in a different business unit or when pursuing a new career path within your current organization may be an option. By networking internally, you can get your name in other people's minds and help them understand your interests and goals.

In the future, there may be an open role that would be a perfect match for you. Even if you don't have the specific qualifications, you'll have made the connections and shown your ability to take initiative. If the hiring manager already has a good understanding of your passions and transferable skills, you're well-positioned to be considered for job openings that may be just outside of your expertise, but for which you have the aptitude or interest.

Internal networking do's

1. Prepare your professional value proposition (PVP): Also called a 30-second elevator pitch, your PVP is compelling, concise and conveys your unique value.
2. Focus on building relationships and helping others across your organization: Get into the right mindset by understanding that networking isn't schmoozing (you're not a car salesman). Networking is strategic with mutually beneficial value involved, so don't forget to ask

what you can do for your contact.

3. Develop a conversational style: Organize your networking by understanding how to build different types of rapport, keep track of what you and your contacts spoke about and be sure to follow up appropriately. Use spreadsheets or online tools to keep administrative notes and for managing contacts.

4. Think creatively about who to network with:

- Coworkers – Create an easy avenue for open dialogues with other employees who you don't get to see very often (or have never even met) so that you can learn more about their roles within the organization.
- Supervisors – Find shared interests or other commonalities that can help you to better relate to your manager or direct report.
- Internal recruiters – Ensure they keep you in the forefront of their minds when they hear about a new role or foresee a need coming up in the organization that would suit your interests.
- People who interact with your company – This can include vendors, suppliers, clients and consultants. They can provide links to other employees in your organization whom you might not know.

Internal networking help the organization: Internal networking develops symbiotic relationships with coworkers and leads to a higher sense of empowerment and personal achievement – improving engagement and longevity with the company along the way. Without internal networking, it's easier for employees to feel disconnected, which can cause performance issues and lead to talent searching for roles outside the organization. Instead of losing employees to other organizations, HR leaders can use the power of cross-company social connections to help employees develop more passion and purpose in their work and a stronger connection to their colleagues. Engaged employees with sociable work environments boost the morale of their coworkers, encourage everyone around them and bring out the best in others. This can lead the organization to outperform competition across every business metric and gain that winning advantage.

Another way internal networking helps the organization is by cultivating satisfied employees who are so well connected and content within the company environment and culture that they'd rather not leave the organization at all. Even if there's a layoff, companies that have a powerful internal network of employee evangelists may see a rise in employees. These are people who have left an organization only to return to work for that same employer. This isn't just beneficial for the employee – who's rehired based on previous experience and reputation – it's also ideal for the organization because it's more cost-effective and efficient to rehire someone with cultural knowledge and internal contacts than to hire someone who's completely new. When employees return, they bring legacy knowledge with them. In other words, they already know what the company is about, and on some level, they're already on board with its mission. This historical knowledge can jumpstart the employee in their new role and make the hiring and onboarding processes much easier.'

HR helps employees network more efficiently:

- Host office events: Put internal networking events on the calendar periodically. They don't have to be only after work hours when you may not have high attendance. Plan something during the work day, even if it's just one hour, to bring people together and promote collaboration and socialization.
- Online groups: Using social media and online business-wide platforms can provide employees with a forum to exchange insights while investing in open communication. The workforce can use digital tools to ask questions, request resources or share information.
- Team motivation: Team events and bonding set the tone for comradely and internal networking by making the workforce feel closer and more nurtured and engaged. Some options include:

  - attending industry events/conferences
  - volunteering
  - local get-togethers or virtual activities
  - educational or networking nights for teams, employee resource groups (ERGs) or employee chapters of larger organizations

- Scheduled breaks: Giving employees time to socialize is important for well-being and is a powerful tool to provide opportunities for them to connect with different people. You can schedule lunches or activities where the workforce has the opportunity to talk with someone new every other month, or team lunches where everyone gets their voice heard. You could also set aside time for new employees to meet with veterans – whether virtually or in person – to learn about the company's culture as well life outside of the organization.

Internal networking is all about conveying value through social relationships. Whether you are in HR or an employee, having internal social connections makes the environment more pleasant and increases the teamwork spirit – ultimately creating a better overall work experience and positive workplace culture.

Barriers to building a Leadership Network

All the following sorts of difference can make Leadership Networking more difficult:

- **Operational differences**: eg adversarial culture, networking being counter-cultural Level differences: networking up/down
- **Demographic differences**: networking with people who differ with respect race, gender, age, county of origin, socioeconomic status
- **Your own personality** / patterns of behaviour.

Critical requirements of leadership networking:

1. Leadership networking demands authenticity: have a genuine objective of building relationships providing support, and accomplishing the work for the benefit of the organisation. Authenticity generates trust. People will see through networking that is self-serving or manipulative.
2. Leadership Networking trades in resources: your resources include information, services, access and power. Know your assets and share/ barter them
3. Leadership Networking calls for thoughtful and deliberate use of power: power is defined as the ability to get things done. In the context of Leadership Networking, there are 3 types of power:

   1. Positive Reputation gives you power
   2. Connections to key influencers and decision makers gives you power
   3. Your involvement with the organisation's more important priorities/ problems gives you power

4. Leadership Networking requires skilful communication: you need to make others aware of what you can offer

5. Leadership Networking calls for savvy negotiating skills
6. Leadership Networking means managing conflict

CHAPTER FOURTEEN

Risk Assessment and Management

Leadership has an important role to play in risk assessment with regard to two particular respects. The first is in relation to the risk assessment process itself, when positive and effective leadership is essential to ensure that the process is carried out effectively. Positive leadership is also required after the risk assessment process has been completed to ensure that the actions necessary to implement the risk assessments are put in place and monitored thereafter. Creating an internal culture that promotes risk management can be equally challenging. One gauge of progress, is whether successful risk management is regarded within the company merely as a nonnegative, or as "a positive thing, an added value." Communication is key, and needs to be encouraged in three directions: top-down, bottom-up, and from the audit committee to the board

The top-down part communicates the company's goals and tools—how we will do it, why we do it—so that everybody knows not only that risk management is supported by the board but also that it is an added value for the group. Bottom-up communication encourages business and functional leaders to "own" risk, understanding that if they raise an issue within their purview, their action will be seen "not as a reason to blame them but rather as an effort to improve and protect the balance sheet of the company." The third circuit ensures that risks detected by the audit committee are brought to the board for discussion and possible action. Communication and reporting standards emerged as a significant focus of concern in the survey. More than one-third of respondents expressed concern that proactive communication, potentially preventing or lessening the impact of a crisis, does not take place in a timely manner during daily operations. More than one in four (27%) expressed concern about the impact of both overrides and work-arounds to existing risk management policies and procedures and of a "good news culture" that prevents management from receiving and absorbing counterintuitive, non-consensus information or views on risk (29%).

If the process of communication, monitoring, and reporting of risk at every level is the "stick" of risk culture, the "carrot, is incentives—"tying risk to hitting your targets for that year. There's obviously a motivation for each person who likes to keep getting a paycheck or a bonus." Organizations have been slow to adopt risk-based incentives as part of compensation. Only 12% of respondents said their organization aligns risk management with executive pay. Of those that do, some said their company had established compensation assessment periods sufficiently long to ensure that sustainable shareholder value is being created, while others said their organization adds claw back provisions to bonuses in case of underperformance.

Incentives work best when the organization can attract and retain staff with risk management capabilities. However, risk accountability is everyone's responsibility, so it's essential to provide risk training across business and functional areas. That hands a strong role to human resources. "HR sometimes is one of the biggest risks. Do we have the talent in place to help manage that risk?' If they are going into a new country or a new product, or competing in an area where they haven't competed before, do they have the right executive-level talent to manage that risk? And that's, I think, a critical question going forward. We also have a lot of awareness activities that are driven by HR. One week will be business continuity management, or internal audit week. And so this awareness keeps risk front and foremost on people's minds, whether through communication or learning development. HR can also play a part in communicating and educating about risk. Often, the learning development function is in HR. For example, you can make available different courses about risk on internal networks.

Leadership during the risk assessment process: Management and in particular senior management must take a lead during the risk assessment process and ensure that they are actively involved in the whole process. Without leadership from management the risk assessment process is less likely to be effective and successful. A senior manager and preferably someone at board level does therefore need to be involved in the risk assessment process from the start. Effective leadership will entail the following elements.

Creating the vision and goals for the risk assessment process: Senior persons need to be able to impress upon those involved in risk assessment the worth of what they are doing and the benefits of what they are involved in. Personal encouragement from senior personnel will ensure that the risk assessment process is meaningful to those involved. They should emphasize that the process is not a paperwork exercise, it is about saving lives and health, and will be beneficial to the organisation.

Develop a plan: Senior managers need to be at the heart of developing a plan to achieve effective risk assessments. This will involve consultation with and the involvement of employees to decide on how the risk assessment process will be tackled and approached.

It is essential to allocate adequate resources for the process if the credibility of the risk assessment process is to be achieved. Clear objectives and targets for the risk assessment process should be established from the outset and only positive leadership can achieve this.

The risk assessment team: Risk assessments are best carried out by a team of persons and senior managers need to take a lead in the selection of the team. Those involved in the process need to be competent to perform risk assessments. It is critical for at least one manager to be involved in the risk assessment process itself. This will not only show management ownership of the risk assessments, but also should ensure easy access by risk assessment teams as required to the relevant departments and sites as well as ensuring co-operation from those areas being assessed.

Leadership following the risk assessment process: The purpose of risk assessments is the prevention of injury and ill health among the workforce and others who might be affected. Consequently, putting into place any measures indicated by the risk assessment is of key importance and can only happen effectively if leadership by senior managers and directors is shown.

Plan

- Examine what needs to be achieved by the risk assessment process.
- Allocate responsibilities for the process and decide how you will measure the achievement of the aims.
- Record the policy for risk assessment and the plan to deliver it.

Do

- Identify the risk profile of the organisation by assessing the risks within the organisation, identifying what could cause harm in the workplace, who it could harm and how, and what needs to be done to manage the risk.
- Decide what the priorities are and identify the greatest and most important risks.
- Organise the organisations activities to deliver the plan.
- Involve workers and communicate, so that everyone is clear on what is needed.
- Develop positive attitudes and behaviours.
- Provide adequate resources, including competent advice where needed.
- Implement the plan.
- Decide on the preventive and protective measures needed and put them in place.
- Train and instruct, to ensure everyone is competent to carry out their work.
- Supervise to make sure that arrangements are followed.

Check

- Measure the achievements and performance against the plan.
- Make sure that your plan has been implemented.
- Assess how well the risks are being controlled and if you are achieving your aims.
- Carry out a formal audit if necessary.
- Investigate the causes of accidents, incidents or near misses in relation to the performed risk assessments.

Act

- Review the performance of the organisation in relation to the plan on risk assessments.
- Learn from accidents and incidents, ill-health data, errors and relevant experience, including from other organisations.
- Revisit plans, policy documents and risk assessments to see if they need updating.
- Take action on lessons learned, including from audit and inspection reports.

Convincing managers to show leadership: Some managers and directors may seem reluctant to show leadership on risk assessment and the management of the process. Senior personnel manage many demands and may feel that the time spent on risk assessment is not cost effective. In some cases, managers and directors may require training in the worth of showing leadership on risk assessment. A number of "off the shelf" training courses provided by different bodies may be used. These include the IOSH Leading Safely course, for example, which lasts about five hours and places emphasis on the role and influence of management leadership on the successful management of health and safety including the provision of risk assessments. As an alternative, tailored courses can be developed specifically for a group of managers and directors to explain the benefits of positive leadership and costs and downside of poor leadership. Such a training course should explore the arguments for positive leadership. These include the following.

The moral case: It is not easy to find organisations where the moral argument for spending on health and safety is the main driver. This is perhaps a sad commentary on the attitudes of some of our managers and directors, but anyone with any first-hand experience of workplace injuries and ill health finds the moral case compelling. People have the right to return home from work safe and sound. The moral case is in reality the strongest of the arguments.

The legal case: The legal consequences of falling foul of the law on health and safety at work are well known. Both criminal proceedings and civil claims can result, leading to fines and compensation payouts. Both fines and compensation awards are increasing and can have a great financial impact when taken with increases in insurance premiums and damage to reputation and similar knock-on costs. Prison sentences are also possible and directors and managers should note that there appears to be an increase in manslaughter cases. This includes both corporate manslaughter and also gross negligence manslaughter.

The economic case: The economic case for leadership on health and safety is overwhelmingly compelling. Current working conditions resulted in an annual cost of 14 billion and these costs can be translated into local costs for individual organisations. Make sure the indirect costs are also taken into account (ie drop in sales due to loss of reputation as much as cost of lost working time).Many directors may believe that their insurance premiums may cover the potential costs of poor health and safety and this is not the case. In fact, the majority of the costs of accidents/incidents and ill health are not covered by insurance. These include:

- effect on morale and loss of goodwill
- loss of skill/experience
- time taken to deal with any incident
- effect on reputation
- stress
- increases in insurance premium, etc.

Forecasting and Mitigating Risk: One of the advantages of creating a risk committee, is much easier to have extended discussions in respect to risk appetite, risk tolerance. Then you can come with a proposal to the board, and it's much easier to make decisions on the basis of the complete facts. Systemic risk management tools and analytics that enable companies to track and analyze risk and then inform risk committee discussions are becoming more commonplace. More than half (56%) of survey respondents said their organization has increased its use of analytics for risk management in the past three years. Among the tools most often cited are risk "heat maps" (41%), key risk indicator scorecards (36%), maps to identify risks inherent in the organization's strategy (30%), scenario analysis and war-gaming (25%), loss forecasting (25%), and loss simulation (24%). For example, a heat map is created each month, circulated to the business and functional owners of risk, and then reported up to senior management once a month and to the board once a quarter. But while "models should drive decision-making, they should not make up our minds for us, "so we use these tools to inform our decisions rather than to actually draw a line in the sand. "A common mistake I see is that people generate a risk map or a risk profile or a risk register, and then they go back and categorize certain things as strategic risks as opposed to financial or IT risks. That doesn't really mean that you've identified strategic risk. Labeling some of the risk you've identified as strategic is not the same as doing serious strategic risk identification. What's most important, said Conrad, is that appropriate metrics are set at the appropriate level of the organization: KPIs are set depending on what objective we're trying to meet. They may be set by the executive level if they're longer term, or they may be set at the individual business or product level. Each group will have different types of KPIs, depending on what they're measuring. This is where you start to dig a little bit deeper in assigning those key risk indicators that can drive your success or failure.

CHAPTER FIFTEEN

Teamwork and Teambuilding

Team building refers to shaping of the team for smooth functioning. Team building as any formal intervention directed toward improving the development and functioning of a work team. Thus, the process of team building aims at enhancing the effectiveness of a team. Pareek Udai has suggested following approaches for team building.

The Johari Window Approach: This approach aims at helping members to express their feelings, opinions reactions and accept feedback from team members. This enhances their sensitivity towards the team members.

The Role Negotiation Approach: This approach focuses on understanding the expectations of the team members and accommodating their behaviour according to the expectations. This enhances the collaborative effort of the team members.

The Team Roles Approach: This approach advocates that there are certain roles which each team members are expected to perform. Belbin has identified eight roles. They are : Chairman/coordinator, shaper, plant, monitor/evaluator, company worker, resource investigator, team worker and completer/finisher. Smooth performance of these roles brings harmony in the effort of the team members.

The Behaviour Modification Approach: This approach focuses on examining members behaviour towards the team. The individual member evaluates his/her own behaviour and finds out the most suitable behaviour. Now he/she adopts the most suitable behaviour for the performance of the team.

The Simulation Approach: In this approach an artificial team is formed where members interact, discuss, deliberate and learn from other members behaviour. In this situation, the team members learn the most effective way of dealing with the challenges and meet the requirements and the expectations of the team members.

The Action Research Approach : In this approach, the whole range of behaviour is analysed and evaluated. The researcher interacts with the team members and evaluates their behaviour. The effort is made to find out most suitable behaviour of the team members.

The Appreciative Inquiry Approach : This approach focuses on the identification of positive qualities in the team members. The effort is made to channelise these positive qualities towards the achievements of the team goal.

Pareek Udai has integrated the above approaches and further suggested following approaches for team

Building which are discussed below : Projection into Future : In this approach, the team members prepare common vision of the team. Several small teams may prepare their own vision which may be further developed as a broader organisational vision.

The team members may be encouraged to make effort towards realising them.

Linkage with Individual Goals: As you must be aware that the building block of the team is individual. Each person has his/her individual goal as well as team goal. Therefore, the individual goal must be integrated with the team goal. This brings harmony in the team effort and enhances the performance of the team.

Force Field Analysis: Several forces influence the performance of the team. Team members are required to analyse these forces and identify the positive forces. These favourable forces are channelised for the achievement of the team goal.

Strengthening Positive Forces: The positive forces are identified and further reinforced. The reinforcement of behaviour motivates the members for making efforts towards the realisation of team goal. This further strengthens the positive behaviour of the team members.

Reducing Negative Forces: In this approach, the forces which inhibit the performance of the team are identified. The efforts are made to remove these negative forces.

Monitoring: The team members chalk out detailed plans and targets to be achieved. The mechanisms for achieving these targets are spelt out. The steps are devised to monitor them at each step. The proper monitoring mechanism facilitates the process of accomplishment of team goal.

While building the team, the managers must take into account those factors which contribute to effective accomplishment of the team goals. The integrated view of the above approaches may provide better insights for enhancing the effectiveness of the team.

CONCEPT OF LEADERSHIP

Leadership may be defined as a process of influencing group activities towards the achievement of certain goals. Thus, the leader is a person in a group who is capable of influencing the group to work willingly. He guides and directs other people and provides purpose and direction to their efforts. The leader is a part of the group that he leads, but he is distinct from the rest of the group. Leadership is the activity of influencing people to strive willingly for group objectives. Leadership naturally implies the existence of a leader and followers as well as their mutual interaction. It involves interpersonal relation, which sustains the followers accepting the leader's guidance for accomplishment of specified goals. Managers have to guide and lead their subordinates towards the achievement of group goals. Therefore, a manager can be more effective if he is a good leader. He does not depend only on his positional power or formal authority to secure group performance but exercises leadership influence for the purpose. As a leader he influences the conduct and behaviour of the members of the work team in the interest of the organisation as well as the individual subordinates and the group as a whole. But leadership and management are not the same thing. Management involves planning, organising, coordinating and controlling operations in achieving various organisational goals. Leadership is the process which influences the people and inspires them to willingly accomplish the organisational objectives. Thus, a manager is more than a leader. On the other hand, a leader need not necessarily be a manager. For instance, in an informal group, the leader may influence the conduct of his fellow members but he may not be a manager. His leadership position is due to the acceptance of his role by his followers. But, the manager, acting as a leader, has powers delegated to him by his superiors. His leadership is an accompaniment of his position as a manager having an organised group of subordinates under his authority. Thus, managerial leadership has the following characteristics.

• It is a continuous process whereby the manager influences, guides and directs the behaviour of subordinates.

• The manager-leader is able to influence his subordinate's behaviour at work due to the quality of his own behaviour as leader.

• The purpose of managerial leadership is to get willing cooperation of the work group in the achievement of specified goals.

• The success of a manager as leader depends on the acceptance of his leadership by the subordinates.

• Managerial leadership requires that while group goals are pursued, individual goals are also achieved.

Team Building Exercises

- **Encourage many trust building exercises in your team. Team members must trust each other for the maximum output.** Blindfold half of your team members and ask them to jump over bricks with the help of members who can see. Repeat this exercise and now blindfold those who could see earlier. This exercise goes a long way in building the trust among the team members. An individual might be a little hesitant initially, but the moment he jumps over the brick with his fellow team member without getting hurt, he starts trusting him. The trust factor increases with time and relations among the team members improve.

- **One must know his fellow team member well.** You can't work with someone you don't know. Include a lot of exercises which help the team members know each other well. Make pairs and ask them to write whatever they know about their partner and vice a versa. You can ask anyone to write his partner's favourite colour, favourite outfit, preferred hangout zone and so on. Ask his partner to correct him if he is wrong in his answers. People know a lot about each other this way and also find out some unknown facts about their partner. Ask the team members to give their introduction one by one once the team is formed.

- **The team members must be compatible with each other. Include icebreaking activities in the team.** Take them out for picnics; get togethers where they can interact with each other freely on any topic. Allow the individuals to bring their families as well. People come a lot closer this way. Relationships improve. Remember your team member's birthday, anniversary or any other important date and do not forget to wish him that day. Ask for a treat! This way, individuals are no longer strangers to each other and the bonding increases.

- **Encourage activities where individuals come together as a single unit and work for a common task.** Collect some even sized sticks, rope, nails, hammer, and glue stick. Ask your team members to construct a bridge out of the sticks using the rope, hammer, gluestick and nails. You will be surprised to see that everyone will be involved in the activity and help each other in making the bridge. The concentration and will power to do something increases and individuals learn to work as a single unit. They all work together, each one contributing something or the other to construct the bridge i.e. accomplish the task assigned to their team.

Why Leaders Need to Encourage and Prioritize Team Building: There's a big difference between being a boss and being a leader. A boss gives orders. A leader provides guidance. Traditional boss-employee relationships typically go like this: A boss tells their employees what to do and when they need to do it, and the employees go and get it done. Instead, the best leaders are the ones who take a teamwork approach to solving problems and completing work-related tasks. Leading doesn't just involve directing but involves teaching the team about how they can best work together. Leaders need to be working towards developing great teams every day. In fact, the ability to build teams is a valuable leadership quality. Leaders who are effective at this have a few essential characteristics. They are good communicators, trustworthy, and they nurture relationships with their employees. Leaders also must be keenly aware of what their team needs to do their best work. And importantly, they understand the strengths and weaknesses of each member and give them each a role in which they can excel. These kinds of leadership qualities can help build motivated and efficient work teams to increase productivity and workplace happiness. Team leaders have a lot of pressure on them. They have to retain a position of authority and respect. They have to inspire a common purpose for the members of their team to agree on and work towards. And they need to be actively involved in developing the skills of individuals on their team so that they can benefit the group. Many people in positions of leadership don't know the best ways to encourage and develop team building among their employees. Team building activities are a great way to get started with this. They help leaders get a better sense of their team's skills and discover how to encourage teamwork on a regular basis.

How Leaders Can Create Fun Team Building Environments: Team building doesn't have to be restricted to regular meetings and day-to-day discussions. The most effective events are the ones that take employees out of the office and put them in new and fun situations. Leaders can treat their employees with activities that will strengthen the daily work they put into building a great team. These kinds of activities can help employees see each other in a new setting, strengthening connections between them.

Challenges also work to expand people's skills when they are faced with new problems to solve.

THE ADVANTAGES AND DISADVANTAGES OF TEAMS: Putting together a team of skilled people may be the best choice for accomplishing a particular task . . . or it may not. Like most other ways of addressing tasks, teams have advantages and disadvantages. Some of their strong points include:

- A team broadens what individuals can do. Team member's gain from the fact that being part of a group makes it possible to do things they couldn't necessarily do alone. A good team supports and enhances the skills and learning of its members, and brings out the best in them. Humans are, after all, social animals, and, as a species, we've worked in teams for a long time. Try killing and butchering a mammoth single-handedly.

- Several heads mean a wider range of ideas. Teams can be more imaginative than individuals, and come at things from a larger number of perspectives.

- Teams can have a greater array of talents and skills than can be found in a single individual. That obviously increases both their effectiveness and the variety of what they can address.

- Team members learn new skills from their colleagues. This increases their own range, and also constantly broadens the team's capabilities.

- Teamwork is more efficient than a number of individuals working solo . The members of a good team know how to assign tasks to the appropriate people, and how to coordinate what they're doing for the maximum effect.

- Teamwork provides relief when someone is having a problem. There is always backup and help available, and the stress is less because you're not the only one doing the job.

- By the same token, the fact that each member knows he's responsible to others works to make him more effective. No one wants to let others down, or to be seen as the weak link. When a team is working well, all its members are aware of their parts in the overall mission, and try to make sure that others' work isn't wasted because of them.

- A team member has more ownership of what she's doing. She's involved in the planning of the team's actions, and she can see how her job fits into the larger purpose of the team and the organization. She doesn't feel like she's working in a vacuum.

- Good teams can build leaders. They give everyone a chance to show what he can do, and to exercise leadership when that's appropriate.
- A shared vision keeps everyone moving forward.

That's a pretty impressive array of strengths, but there are weaknesses as well.

- Team decision-making takes longer than individual decision-making, and can be a great deal more difficult.
- Depending upon the task or problem, team effort can be wasted effort. Some things can be more easily dealt with by individuals.
- The team's success may hang on the work of the weakest or least effective team member.
- Once a team gets rolling in a particular direction, even if it's the wrong direction, it develops momentum. It may be harder for a team than for an individual to get back on a better track.
- Especially at the beginning when members are still getting familiar with one another, the work of teams can bog down in interpersonal issues, resentments, and blame.
- On the other hand, once team members are bonded and committed to one another and the team, they may be reluctant to tell others when their work is unsatisfactory or to point out that the team isn't getting anywhere.
- Individuals on the team may lose motivation because of the lack of individual recognition for the value of their work. The balance between team effort and individual recognition is a delicate one.

HOW DO YOU BUILD A TEAM?

Building a good team involves a great deal more than simply choosing members. That's only the first step, and you may not even have the chance to do that if you're working with an already-existing group. Developing and communicating a vision, planning the team's mission to match the vision, working out how people will function together, and then fine-tuning it over time are only some of the other elements of team building. The following are guidelines, and are not meant to be a step-by-step guide to team building. Some elements of the process may get worked out over time in the course of the team's activities. Others may reach critical points and be dealt with then. Each team is unique, and there is no single formula for success or excellence.

CHOOSING TEAM MEMBERS

Whether you're hiring new staff people especially for a team, or choosing from among the existing staff members of an organization, there are a number of factors to consider.

- **Start with the best people you can find.** No team is any better than its members, and finding the best people for the jobs at hand is tremendously important. "Best " doesn't always simply mean someone who can do the work better than anyone else, however. Someone may be a terrific practitioner, but difficult to work with, or jealous of others' successes. It may make more sense to choose someone who's only second best (although still very good) at the work, but better at being a member of a team.

- **Choose team members so they'll have a good fit.** The issue of fit was mentioned earlier, and it can't be overstressed. In order for team members to fit together well, they must connect on a number of levels.

  - *Personality.* People don't necessarily need to become best friends, but they need at least to respect, and, better yet, to like one another. They're going to be spending a lot of time together: it's far more conducive to the team's success if time spent together is seen as pleasant. In addition, the more people like and respect one another, the more they'll communicate, and the more loyalty they'll feel to the team and its work. Both of these conditions add to the effectiveness of the team. As team members are chosen, therefore, it's essential to consider whether each person is likely to get along well with the others, and what she'll add to or take away from the personality of the team.

  - *World view.* Especially in health, human service, and community work, it's important that the overall goals of everyone involved be similar. If some team members see participant empowerment as paramount, and others see participants as annoying and obstructive, there will be friction. Not only will team members disagree and perhaps work against one another, but the whole purpose of the team's work will be weakened. It's vital, therefore, that the basic vision of the team's purpose be shared. In choosing team members, people's attitudes and general world views need to play a large role.

○ *Work ethic.* Team members don't have to be workaholics, but they need to have similar work ethics and similar conceptions of what doing a good job means. If that 's the case, then no one will get upset because he's doing more work than others, or because one person isn't pulling his weight.

○ *Ability to use disagreement and conflict well.* Team members need to be able to disagree positively, and to use their disagreements and differences about the work to come up with better solutions. They have to be willing to voice those disagreements, because disagreement is often a wellspring for good ideas. At the same time, they have to be able to remove such disagreements from the personal, and look at them as problems to be solved with creativity and mutual respect.

- **Look for members with a diversity of backgrounds and perspectives.** It seems obvious that the more different frames of reference that can be brought to bear on an issue or a community, the better. Teams that are diverse in a number of ways -- background, training, culture, etc. -- bring a range of skills and perspectives to the work they do. Choosing team members with an eye for what they bring to the mix can create a more dynamic and creative group.

- **Look for members with a commitment to the concept of working as a team.** Teamwork often requires that people put aside their individual interests in order to accomplish the team's goals. Team members need to understand just what it means to work as part of a team. They have to be willing to compromise -- especially when they know they 're right -- and to maintain a team atmosphere of civility and mutual respect. More to the point, they have to check their egos at the door if the team is to work well.

- **Look for team members committed the team's guiding vision.** The vision may be one that's jointly developed (see below), or it may already exist before the team is formed. In either case, belief in it and a willingness to strive toward its realization are a large part of what will make a team successful in the long run. Anyone you choose needs to have the passion needed to make that kind of commitment, and the sense of the world that will allow commitment to the team's particular vision.

- **Find people with a sense of humor.** The work of community-based and grass roots organizations and initiatives is always hard, often frustrating, and seldom pays well, if at all. People need a sense of humor and fun attitude to maintain their enthusiasm, and to deal with the disappointments or failures that are an inevitable part of even the most successful efforts. The gallows humor that some people find appalling in health and human service situations is often just as necessary to the smooth functioning of the organization as the competence and devotion of the staff in the work they do.

A team is more than just a group of people working together toward a common goal. It's a group that functions as a single unit, working toward a powerful shared vision of accomplishment. In situations where teams are called for, a team that works well can accomplish more than all of its individual members working alone, because each member's work supports and complements the others'. Building a team involves both choosing the members (if you have that option), and forging those individuals into a working unit. That involves thinking about how people fit together, and helping them to establish group and individual bonds.

Team building also requires looking at the characteristics of good teams. It means providing or generating with the team at the outset a vision that everyone can be passionate about. The next step is clearly defining the concept of a team, and making sure everyone knows how he fits into that concept. Once that's in place, the team needs to plan jointly how it will function (who will do what, how everyone will communicate effectively, what the team's norms will be). Any personal issues need to be addressed at the beginning and resolved as quickly as possible. Teams need to examine their work and understand the reasons for successes and failures, so they can continue to improve and develop. Teams need recognition for their accomplishments, so they'll know their work is appreciated. If you can build a team of good people using these guidelines, the achievement of your goals is practically in the bag.